EXPOSITORY THOUGHTS ON ACTS

A SURGEON LOOKS AT A
PHYSICIAN'S NARRATIVE

Expository thoughts on Acts

Expository Thoughts on Acts

*A Surgeon looks at a
Physician's narrative*

by Jonathan Redden

Christian Year Publications

ISBN-13: 978 1 872734 39 2

Typeset by John Ritchie Ltd., Kilmarnock
Printed by Bell & Bain Ltd., Glasgow

Contents

Preface

It is over 150 years since J. C. Ryle wrote "Expository thoughts on the Gospels". These monumental works have remained in print and popular amongst Christian preachers and readers alike. Although he was a prolific writer, he did not turn his hand to write an exposition of "Acts".

Ryle was essentially a humble man, but his style was readable, even to modern generations, clear, trenchant and direct, to the point of being dogmatic and decidedly Protestant. Yet he demonstrated to his readers clear sympathy concerning human griefs, failings and weaknesses.

It is not possible and would be foolish to try and imitate another person's style but I have used his format of taking a passage and writing some thoughts on it.

It is intentionally not an academic, critical evaluation of the text, but more focused on application, which I hope groups and individual readers alike will find helpful.

It is written with a classic evangelical view of the inspiration of scripture. I do acknowledge that that there are now many early Greek manuscripts available and these do contain some variations in the text. Nevertheless, these variations are small and do not affect a single doctrine or precept in the whole of the New Testament.

I appreciate that there are recent scholars who have questioned Luke's authorship of Acts. However, the authorship is supported by a process of examining the characters of Acts and Paul's letters, and by a method of elimination, the most likely candidate is Luke. Furthermore, early Church Fathers including Irenaeus point to Luke's authorship.

As a surgeon, I have always been fascinated by the person of Luke the physician. He was described by Paul as the beloved physician. (Col. 4:14) Luke was loyal to the apostle and stayed resolutely with Paul when all the others had left him. (2 Tim. 4:11) As a Christian physician with a compassionate heart he would have had profound insights into human nature and personality.

In the long and varied history of medicine, there has been a friendly rivalry and banter between surgeons and physicians, but Christian doctors have always had an affinity for this most godly and conscientious of physicians. Luke, led by the Holy Spirit crafted two literary and theological masterpieces when he wrote his gospel and The Acts of the Apostles. There have been with reason numerous commentaries on Luke's work, but as far as I know, none of those published has been written by a surgeon.

It has to be admitted that there is little new to say about Acts and I have consulted numerous texts and commentaries. It is with gratitude that I have been able to include them in the bibliography. They have all been most helpful.

The narrative of Acts demonstrates a vivid picture of the early church. Luke describes successes and crises. However, with the resolution of each crisis, the work of God moved forward. Present day Christians would learn much from the love, patience, commitment and suffering of these early Apostles, pioneers and their friends.

I am grateful to my friends, and the staff of the publishers, Ritchie Media, Alison Banks, Alan Cameron and Fraser Munro, and particularly Jane my wife for their encouragement and comments.

It is our prayer that those who read these thoughts will be helped and strengthened in their Christian journey. If there are readers who have not yet committed themselves to Christ in a personal way, I hope that they will be enabled to copy the example of these women and men of "Acts" and Christians down the centuries and say yes to the invitation of Jesus to follow Him.

Bibliography

Barker, Kenneth, (Ed.) *The NIV Study Bible* (London: Hodder and Stoughton, 1990)

Bruce, F. F., *The Acts of the Apostles* (London: The Tyndale Press, 1965)

Calvin, John, *The Acts of the Apostles 1-13* (Edinburgh: Oliver and Boyd, 1965)

Calvin, John, *The Acts of the Apostles 14-28* (Edinburgh: Oliver and Boyd, 1965)

Dunn, James D. G. *The Christ and the Spirit, Volume 2 Pneumatology* (Grand Rapids: WM. B. Eerdmans Publishing Co., 1998)

Gaukroger, Stephen, *Acts: Free to Live* (Nottingham: Crossway Books, 1993)

MacArthur, John, *The MacArthur Study Bible* (Nashville: Thomas Nelson, 1997)

Neil, William, *The Acts of the Apostles* (London: Marshall, Morgan & Scott, 1973)

Pawson, David, *A Commentary on Acts* (Ashford: Anchor Recordings Ltd, 2014)

Pollock, John, *The Apostle, A Life of Paul* (Colorado Springs: David C. Cook, 2012)

Rackham, R. B., *The Acts of the Apostles* (London: Methuen and Co. ltd, 1957)

Ryle, J. C., *Expository thoughts on Luke, volume 1* (Edinburgh: The Banner of Truth Trust, 1986)

Ryle, J. C., *Expository thoughts on Luke, volume 2* (Edinburgh: Banner of Truth Trust, 1986)

Stott, John, *The Message of Acts* (Nottingham: Inter-Varsity Press, 2013)

Williams, C. S. C., *The Acts of the Apostles* (London: A. and C. Black, 1957)

Williams, Peter, *Acts: Church on the Move* (Leominster: Day One Publications, 2004)

Wright, Tom, *Acts for Everyone, Part 1* (London: Society for Promoting Christian Knowledge, 2008)

Wright, Tom, *Acts for Everyone, Part 2* (London: Society for Promoting Christian Knowledge, 2008)

Acts 1:1-5

1 The former account I made, O Theophilus, of all that Jesus began both to do and teach, 2 until the day in which He was taken up, after He through the Holy Spirit had given commandments to the apostles whom He had chosen, 3 to whom He also presented Himself alive after His suffering by many infallible proofs, being seen by them during forty days and speaking of the things pertaining to the kingdom of God. 4 And being assembled together with them, He commanded them not to depart from Jerusalem, but to wait for the Promise of the Father, "which," He said, "you have heard from Me; 5 for John truly baptized with water, but you shall be baptized with the Holy Spirit not many days from now.

Luke begins Acts with references to his former book, the third Gospel, and his Patron, Theophilus. He has already described how he obtained his information in his first book, and here he goes straight into a link between the first and the second. We would do well to note that Luke is concerned with data and facts to relate the story. He does not define a series of precepts. He does not proclaim a series of oracles or well-intentioned intellectual philosophies, but is concerned about what his key characters did and said in a well organised readable narrative. Acts was written by Luke, a physician, historian, theologian and more importantly, he was inspired by the Holy Spirit.

We are reminded of what Jesus did and taught. Before being taken up to heaven, He left instructions through the Holy Spirit. In the book of Acts the presence of Jesus and the influence of the Holy Spirit are evident throughout this dramatic account.

One may wonder what Jesus taught in the six weeks after His resurrection. We know only a fragment, but in the course of a few weeks, a remarkable change took place in the disciples. They changed from a squabbling, spiritually weak, and insecure group to a purposeful, confident and knowledgeable band, who would spread a good news message that has transformed the world.

God would no longer be remote, only knowable to a few. From then on, He would be available to all. There would be no need for a continued sacrificial system and all the temple priests and rituals. Jesus had provided on the cross a full and complete sacrifice for sin. Furthermore, Christ would be with, and in, the believer through the person of the Holy Spirit.

The Gospel of Luke moves on quickly to an account of the humble circumstances surrounding the birth of John the Baptist and the Lord Jesus. Acts has a statement about our Lord's ascension. From a humble birth, Jesus is declared Lord of heaven and earth. He stands in glory and victory and makes intercession for us.

There are a number of points to learn from this passage. Firstly, we learn that there are numerous proofs concerning the resurrection of Christ. (v 3) Many have tried to disprove the resurrection with a number of alternatives, but none has stood up to proper scrutiny. Suffice to say that we can believe that Jesus rose again from the dead with good reason, and with an assurance that gives great comfort to a Christian. This is particularly true during times of trial, severe illness, and under the "shadow of death". (Ps. 23: 4)

Secondly, we are reminded that the mission that first began with Jesus the Son of God continues but this time through the agency of these unlikely apostles. The call to mission would soon extend to all believers. It is extraordinary to think that Christ still commissions people like us to extend His purposes and spread the knowledge and truth of Him throughout the world. It is even more remarkable to note that despite the variable efforts and shortcomings of fallible people, His overall purposes will never fail.

Thirdly, we note that the apostles had to wait in Jerusalem. There are times when we have to wait before we move into some form of occupation or service. Some become impatient and may even lose heart, but we need to remain faithful and expectant. Whilst we may be waiting for the big task, we can always be reassured that there are seemingly small tasks to do, which are no less important to God.

Acts 1:6-11

6 Therefore, when they had come together, they asked Him, saying, "Lord, will You at this time restore the kingdom to Israel?" 7 And He said to them, "It is not for you to know times or seasons which the Father has put in His own authority. 8 But you shall receive power when the Holy Spirit has come upon you; and you shall be witnesses to Me in Jerusalem, and in all Judea and Samaria, and to the end of the earth." 9 Now when He had spoken these things, while they watched, He was taken up, and a cloud received Him out of their sight. 10 And while they looked steadfastly toward heaven as He went up, behold, two men stood by them in white apparel, 11 who also said, "Men of Galilee, why do you stand gazing up into heaven? This same Jesus, who was taken up from you into heaven, will so come in like manner as you saw Him go into heaven."

We continue this section on the time between our Lord's resurrection and ascension when Jesus gave His final teaching and instructions to His beloved disciples. In his gospel account, Luke informs us that Jesus:

Opened their understanding, that they might comprehend the Scriptures. Then He said to them, "Thus it is written, and thus it was necessary for the Christ to suffer and to rise from the dead the third day, and that repentance and remission of sins should be preached in His name to all nations, beginning at Jerusalem (Luke 24: 45-47)

They asked Jesus a question that had preoccupied so many minds at that time, "Lord, are you at this time going to restore the kingdom to Israel?" (v 6).

This is also a question in modern times that has intrigued students, concerning the present physical and political state of Israel.

The contemporary Israel has been described as a subject of end-time prophecy, and may indeed be of profound significance. It should be enough to humbly accept that it was neither for the disciples nor for us to know the precise timing.The reply given about dates, and that only God knows them, indicates that there are other priorities, which His people need to pursue. They were to receive power to be witnesses, and for that they would be given Holy Spirit power. They were to witness from Jerusalem to the ends of the earth. Two thousand years later, and with a world population of over seven billion, that kingdom still expands.

The power that Jesus will give to His disciples is that given by the Holy Spirit. It would be the power of speech and the performance of signs. It is also the power to cope with all the trials that would fall on them. (Acts 4:8) It is the power to love, be joyful, peaceful, patient, kind, good, faithful, gentle, and self-controlled. (Gal 5:22) It is not power to domineer or to control others in order to achieve status or rank. It is to be used to the benefit of others and God's glory. Many pastors, priests and prelates have misused their position to manipulate, abuse and to destroy. (3 John 9) Thankfully, there are more who have been used by God to warn, encourage and build up.

Jesus was then taken up into heaven. (v 9) We cannot and will not understand the physics and chemistry of this event. The disciples were certainly awestruck as, "They were looking intently up into the sky." (v 10) It is a mystery only known to God. Nevertheless, we do know that on a certain day, Jesus will come back in the same way. When Jesus first came, it was in humble circumstances, "born of a woman, born under the law", (Gal 4:4) and placed in an animal food trough. Only a few, including some shepherds, were aware of His coming, only a few acknowledged who He is during His ministry on Earth. When He comes a second time, He will come in great glory, and all will have to acknowledge Him for whom He is, the Saviour of humankind, and the King of all the universe. There will also be great regret, sorrow and judgement of unbelievers who will "Look on Him whom they pierced." (John 19:37, cf. Rev 1:7).

Modern preachers would do well to speak more frequently about the second coming than they generally do.

Acts 1:12-14

12 Then they returned to Jerusalem from the mount called Olivet, which is near Jerusalem, a Sabbath day's journey. **13** And when they had entered, they went up into the upper room where they were staying: Peter, James, John, and Andrew; Philip and Thomas; Bartholomew and Matthew; James the son of Alphaeus and Simon the Zealot; and Judas the son of James. **14** These all continued with one accord in prayer and supplication, with the women and Mary the mother of Jesus, and with His brothers.

The return of the disciples to Jerusalem shows a deep renewal of spirit and unity. This contrasts markedly with the past when they were rivals and self-seeking, of little faith, deserting and lying to avoid trouble. This list of disciples names eleven faithful men who were accompanied by over a hundred fellow believers.

We learn a number of points from these three verses.

The first point is that ministers of God and all faithful believers should be men and women of prayer. Many a ministry has gone awry because of lack of prayer, and fruitful ministries have been accompanied by much time spent in prayer. Jesus spent a night in prayer before His original appointment of the apostles. Such was the measure and impact of His prayer life that His disciples asked Him to teach them how to pray. (Luke 11:1)

The second point is that even the most stubborn and unbelieving family members can be converted and become shining witnesses. The Gospel narratives tell us that Jesus' "brothers did not believe in Him." (John 7:5). However, the risen Lord appeared to James who later became a leader of the church in Jerusalem. James and his brother Jude wrote epistles, which became part of the New Testament.

Unbelief of family members can be a great heartache and sorrow, but we should never give up praying for them. There are numerous stories of family who have come to Christ after many years of persistent prayer.

The third point is that Luke, as in his Gospel, referred to the women who were part of the faithful community. He gives them a status few other ancient writers give them, a status given to them by our Lord Himself. Christian men should respect the role of women in the church. Sadly, the history of the world is littered with episodes when men have abused women.

The fourth point is that this is the last named reference to Mary in the New Testament. We should admire her, copy her spirit of obedience and call her blessed, and may even name places of worship, schools, hospitals and streets after her. However, nowhere in the Bible is she referred to as, 'The Queen of Heaven", co-redemptrix, or a mediator. Such titles and veneration are a dangerous accretion to Christianity. They make Jesus more remote and diminish His lordship. He is the one who was tempted and yet without sin. He alone sympathises and makes intercession for us. (Heb 7: 25)

The final short point is that although we may begin with weak and faltering faith, it can grow and grow if we are obedient and follow Him conscientiously.

Acts 1:15-26

15 And in those days Peter stood up in the midst of the disciples (altogether the number of names was about a hundred and twenty), and said, **16** "Men and brethren, this Scripture had to be fulfilled, which the Holy Spirit spoke before by the mouth of David concerning Judas, who became a guide to those who arrested Jesus; **17** for he was numbered with us and obtained a part in this ministry." **18** (Now this man purchased a field with the wages of iniquity; and falling headlong, he burst open in the middle and all his entrails gushed out. **19** And it became known to all those dwelling in Jerusalem; so that field is called in their own language, Akel Dama, that is, Field of Blood.) **20** "For it is written in the book of Psalms: 'Let his dwelling place be desolate, And let no one live in it'; and, 'Let another take his office.' **21** "Therefore, of these men who have accompanied us all the time that the Lord Jesus went in and out among us, **22** beginning from the baptism of John to that day when He was taken up from us, one of these must become a witness with us of His resurrection." **23** And they proposed two: Joseph called Barsabas, who was surnamed Justus, and Matthias. **24** And they prayed and said, "You, O Lord, who know the hearts of all, show which of these two You have chosen **25** to take part in this ministry and apostleship from which Judas by transgression fell, that he might go to his own place." **26** And they cast their lots, andthe lot fell on Matthias. And he was numbered with the eleven apostles.

During their time of waiting, the faithful were not idle and Peter addressed them with real confidence and authority. He had to deal with the gap created by the betrayal and suicide of Judas Iscariot. He pointed out that an apostle must have been with them from the beginning of Jesus' ministry, and be a witness to the resurrection. Little is known of Joseph or the elected Mathias, but we can be assured that they were faithful witnesses.

The portion which is an account of the last moments on earth of Judas Iscariot should fill us with sadness and dread. It seems that the whole of Jerusalem were aware of his shocking demise.

As one of the twelve, he was given great privileges, and he saw at first hand the character and miracles of Jesus. And yet with all this, he was an apostate and a robber who was quite prepared to steal from the common funds. He was given opportunities to be restored and yet, he allowed the devil to enter him. (John 13: 27) This should be a warning never to trifle with the devil and never to dabble with evil. Playing with Ouija boards, attending séances, reading horoscopes and the like, can only lead to personal harm, and should be decidedly avoided.

We should also remember that membership or leadership in a church does not necessarily confer a Christian character or true conversion. Sometimes, and fortunately, in only a few cases, individuals are prepared to misuse their position to the detriment and scandal of the church, and to their own 'shipwreck' and perdition. Some modern writers have attempted to rehabilitate the reputation of Judas Iscariot. It has to be said that there is no scriptural warrant for this revision whatsoever.

Peter was able to interpret scriptural references to the betrayal and betrayer of Jesus. We should note that Peter explicitly affirmed the inspiration of scripture by the Holy Spirit. The inspiration of the Hebrew Scriptures is also clear from Jesus' own ministry and the testimony of all the New Testament. Our response to any preaching should be: "Does this agree with what the Holy Spirit has said in the Bible?"

There are those who have claimed the Spirit's gifting but have sadly called into question Scripture's authority and inspiration.

Acts 2:1-13

1 When the Day of Pentecost had fully come, they were all with one accord in one place. **2** And suddenly there came a sound from heaven, as of a rushing mighty wind, and it filled the whole house where they were sitting. **3** Then there appeared to them divided tongues, as of fire, and one sat upon each of them. **4** And they were all filled with the Holy Spirit and began to speak with other tongues, as the Spirit gave them utterance. **5** And there were dwelling in Jerusalem Jews, devout men, from every nation under heaven. **6** And when this sound occurred, the multitude came together, and were confused, because everyone heard them speak in his own language. **7** Then they were all amazed and marveled, saying to one another, "Look, are not all these who speak Galileans? **8** And how is it that we hear, each in our own language in which we were born? **9** Parthians and Medes and Elamites, those dwelling in Mesopotamia, Judea and Cappadocia, Pontus and Asia, **10** Phrygia and Pamphylia, Egypt and the parts of Libya adjoining Cyrene, visitors from Rome, both Jews and proselytes, **11** Cretans and Arabs--we hear them speaking in our own tongues the wonderful works of God." **12** So they were all amazed and perplexed, saying to one another, "Whatever could this mean?

This day of Pentecost should be celebrated as one of the greatest days in the history of the world. Those who read this passage should feel a sense of joy and excitement. Joy, because the Holy Spirit, who was once only available to a limited few is now given to all who believe and put their trust in Christ. Excitement, because this small band of believers would become a growing world-wide church. How sad it is that fewer and fewer people in the West know of it or want to know anything about this day.

There are a number of lessons that we can learn.

In the first place, the gift of tongues shocked all the God-fearing Jews from various parts of the world because they heard the wonderful works of God in their own language. In the past, the Hebrew language was the only liturgical language. Hebrew was the only language of praise. The emphasis here is that the praise of God may be uttered in any language or dialect. Quality of speech and diction is of some importance, but the most important thing to God is the sincerity of heart. (Acts 13: 22)

Furthermore, those who spoke were Galileans who usually spoke with their marked Northern accent. God can and frequently does use the least expected people to proclaim His wonders rather than the most able and academic. The primary qualification of a Christian witness is to be called by God.

We can note in the second place, the unifying effect of them: "Everyone heard them speak in his own language." (v 6) This was a reverse of the curse of the tower of Babel story recorded in the early chapters of Genesis. In that story, the inhabitants of the earth wanted to make a name for themselves, and glorify their own abilities by building a great tower that would reach into the sky. God's judgement came upon them and nations and peoples were divided due to their sudden different languages. The gift of tongues or languages described here was a reversal of that curse. (Gen 11: 1-9)

In today's world of rapid travel, it is wonderful to visit churches all over the world. Although we still may not be able to understand their language, there is a welcome and unifying fellowship experienced in no other group. I have experienced the common bond of sport, and the common identity and concerns of medics from all over world. However, nowhere else is the same love and oneness in Christ, which is found in true Christian fellowship. That unity was forged on the day of Pentecost.

We are able to note in the third place that wherever God's work is in action, there will be scoffers nearby, who are ready to use any pretext however unlikely to pour scorn on the praise, beliefs, and works of God-inspired Christians. The first jibe was that they were drunk.

Today the scoffers have expanded their invective. It is insinuated by a modern and leading atheist that those Christians who claim to believe in the creative works of God are stupid, ignorant or even wicked. Christians need to admit our mistakes and even wrongdoing. We mourn the scandals that stain God's church. However, the blessings brought to humanity by the work of God's people in all aspects of life appear to be wilfully forgotten by our critics. Our Lord suffered abuse from critics who hated Him without "cause" (John 15: 25). He told us that we should expect a similar response from the world. We need to remember and take comfort from the fact that where there is persecution there may be an accompanying, paradoxical strengthening of the church. We also need to remember to pray for all who suffer persecution. It may be subtle psychological persecution as in the West or more physical persecution as in other parts of the world. It seems that in recent times, more have died for their faith than at any other period of history.

Acts 2:14-41

14 But Peter, standing up with the eleven, raised his voice and said to them, "Men of Judea and all who dwell in Jerusalem, let this be known to you, and heed my words. **15** For these are not drunk, as you suppose, since it is only the third hour of the day. **16** But this is what was spoken by the prophet Joel: **17** 'And it shall come to pass in the last days, says God, That I will pour out of My Spirit on all flesh; Your sons and your daughters shall prophesy, Your young men shall see visions, Your old men shall dream dreams. **18** And on My menservants and on My maidservants I will pour out My Spirit in those days; And they shall prophesy. **19** I will show wonders in heaven above And signs in the earth beneath: Blood and fire and vapor of smoke. **20** The sun shall be turned into darkness, And the moon into blood, Before the coming of the great and awesome day of the Lord. **21** And it shall come to pass That whoever calls on the name of the Lord Shall be saved.' **22** "Men of Israel, hear these words: Jesus of Nazareth, a Man attested by God to you by miracles, wonders, and signs which God did through Him in your midst, as you yourselves also know-- **23** Him, being delivered by the determined purpose and foreknowledge of God, you have taken by lawless hands, have crucified, and put to death; **24** whom God raised up, having loosed the pains of death, because it was not possible that He should be held by it. **25** For David says concerning Him: 'I foresaw the Lord always before my face, For He is at my right hand, that I may not be shaken. **26** Therefore my heart rejoiced, and my tongue was glad; Moreover my flesh also will rest in hope. **27** For You will not leave my soul in Hades, Nor will You allow Your Holy One to see corruption. **28** You have made known to me the ways of life; You will make me full of joy in Your presence.' **29** "Men and brethren, let me speak freely to you of the patriarch David, that he is both dead and buried, and his tomb is with us to this day. **30** Therefore, being a prophet, and knowing that God had sworn with an oath to him that of the fruit of his body, according to the flesh, He would raise up the Christ to sit on his throne, **31** he, foreseeing this, spoke concerning the resurrection of the Christ, that His soul was not left in Hades, nor did His flesh see corruption. **32** This Jesus God has raised up, of which we are all witnesses. **33** Therefore being exalted to the right hand of God, and having received from the Father the promise of the Holy Spirit, He poured out this which you now see and hear. **34** For David did not ascend into the heavens, but he says himself: 'The Lord said to my Lord, "Sit at My right hand, **35** Till I make Your enemies Your footstool."

36 "Therefore let all the house of Israel know assuredly that God has made this Jesus, whom you crucified, both Lord and Christ." **37** Now when they heard this, they were cut to the heart, and said to Peter and the rest of the apostles, "Men and brethren, what shall we do?" **38** Then Peter said to them, "Repent, and let every one of you be baptized in the name of Jesus Christ for the remission of sins; and you shall receive the gift of the Holy Spirit. **39** For the promise is to you and to your children, and to all who are afar off, as many as the Lord our God will call." **40** And with many other words he testified and exhorted them, saying, "Be saved from this perverse generation." **41** Then those who gladly received his word were baptized; and that day about three thousand souls were added to them.

Acts is a book that contains sermons, or rather summaries of sermons. They are direct, dynamic, clear, incisive, and challenge the listener and reader to make a response. Nowhere can they be accused of being boring. Nowhere are they irrelevant. Peter, here, provides a model for subsequent generations of Christian preachers, be it in a large cathedral, a small rural church or meeting place.

Peter appealed to his hearers' natural reason, and interspersed this with quotations from Scripture in order to drive home his point. It could be said that his sermon is an exposition from a passage in the book of Joel.

He appealed to their reason in order to make his defence. The speaking in tongues of the wonderful works of God was not due to new wine, because it was only nine o'clock in the morning. His audience would be fully aware that practising Jews would not drink early in the day. His second appeal to reason came later in the sermon when he made a challenge about the resurrection of Jesus. He said that everyone agreed that Jesus was crucified, for which all the people in Jerusalem bore some responsibility. That was a given. He said that King David's tomb was present here in Jerusalem, which everyone could see. The implication was that the tomb where the body of Jesus was placed was empty. He then arrested their minds by stating that he and the people around him were witnesses of the fact of the resurrection. They had seen Jesus alive.

Peter employed Scripture with great power. The recent events of the death, resurrection and ascension were all prophesied hundreds of years before. The Jews claimed to believe the Scriptures and therefore all that has happened was all part of God's plan.

Modern preachers should be aware, more than ever, of the world and people around them, and should appeal to their natural understanding. They should quote and handle Scripture with great sensitivity and prayer. Even if people claim to not believe the Bible, the words of Scripture still have power to convict and change. It has been said that a preacher should preach with a newspaper in one hand and a Bible in the other. There is much truth in that but it needs to be remembered that of the two, the Bible is by far the more important document.

Sermons should leave hearers with something to ponder, something to do, perhaps even a radical change, as in the case here. The crowd needed to repent, be baptised, and they would receive the gift of the Holy Spirit. We need to take note that all may not be equally filled by the Holy Spirit but all who truly trust in Christ have received the Holy Spirit. In this regard there are not two classes of Christian, those who have received the Holy Spirit and those who have not. Teaching about such a division can and has given great anguish to sensitive souls. In the same way, we should not at any point think that we have it all, and have no need of further infilling by the Holy Spirit.

Peter shared his heart and showed great love for his hearers when he warned and pleaded with them. We also have in verse 39, a wonderful reminder of God's sovereignty in His call to those who are to be members of His church.

There were many thousands in Jerusalem on that day, and only a fraction became believers. No doubt some of them would have been witnesses of Jesus' ministry. At any rate, three thousand converts is a massive response in anyone's book. It was the first in a continuing response we see even to this day. We may come to faith in thousands or in ones and twos, but each one is known, cared for, and loved by God in equal measure. Furthermore, each conversion brings great joy to God. (Luke 15: 7)

Having read this first sermon in Acts, we should ask ourselves the question, have we repented of our sins? Do we accept that

Jesus' death paid the just penalty for our sin when He died on the cross? Do we believe in the resurrection of Jesus? We should not be complacent or rest until we know and believe in our hearts the truths of these statements.

Acts 2:42-47

42 And they continued steadfastly in the apostles' doctrine and fellowship, in the breaking of bread, and in prayers. 43 Then fear came upon every soul, and many wonders and signs were done through the apostles. 44 Now all who believed were together, and had all things in common, 45 and sold their possessions and goods, and divided them among all, as anyone had need. 46 So continuing daily with one accord in the temple, and breaking bread from house to house, they ate their food with gladness and simplicity of heart, 47 praising God and having favor with all the people. And the Lord added to the church daily those who were being saved.

In this short passage we have a vivid picture of the life of the first community of believers. Every Christian and, in particular, every Christian leader should mark well the quality of fellowship that is described here.

Firstly, they not only listened to the apostles' teaching, they devoted themselves to it. Happy is the Christian who delights in the truths of the gospel, whose heart is warmed by the stories of the Bible. Today, through the availability of the Scriptures, Christian books, commentaries in both hard and paperback and electronic forms, we have an access to Christian material unparalleled in human history. Let us endeavour not to lose our enthusiasm or become lukewarm to the content of God's Word.

Secondly, there was a delightful, kind and caring fellowship. This was a selfless kind of fellowship. People sold their goods and shared with those in need.

It was not a Christian communism reminiscent of some compulsive Marxist formula. It was a voluntary giving. People still retained some property and many of them remained home-owners. This selfless love, so rare in a Godless world, was one of the great attractions of Christianity and where practised remains so to this day. Tertullian, the early church father, noted a remark made by onlookers, "See how they love one another."

This love was a continuation, albeit imperfect, of that love demonstrated during the whole of Jesus' ministry. Jesus was the friend of sinners. He met with them and ate with them. He had compassion on the multitude. Jesus wept at the tomb of Lazarus. All Christians need to carry at the front of our minds that, "God so loved the world that He gave His only begotten Son." (John 3: 16}

Thirdly, most commentators agree that the breaking of bread referred to in this passage is an early reference to the Lord's Supper. It was celebrated regularly. It is important that all Christians should remember in this way the significance and reality of our Lord's death and passion. "The bread which we break, is it not the communion of the body of Christ?" (1 Cor. 10:16) Generally speaking, Christian leaders have few worries over those who attend regularly. The book of Hebrews reminds us that we should not absent ourselves from Christian gatherings as some have done. (Heb. 10: 25)

We also need to take to heart that the preaching or teaching of the Apostles and the Lord's Supper were not performances, events or entertainment but true worship.

Fourthly, prayer, and the prayer meeting were another prominent feature of the early church. They prayed in the temple, synagogues and one another's homes. It can be said that prayer is one of the most vital and most neglected aspects of modern Christian life. We should remember that when we pray, God acts. It may be in a most unexpected way and even hard way but God acts. God often allows hardships and heartbreaks in order to drive us to prayer. It is not about getting God to do what we want, but allowing God to do in us what He wants. And that is also ultimately, for His glory and our blessing. Everyone was filled with awe by all that had happened, all that God is, and all that He has done. We do not see here any flippancy or trivialisation, which is so often a characteristic of modern communications and media.

Fifthly, this love, this joy, this awe, was attractive to many outside and each day was marked by the arrival of new converts. The revival described here has been repeated although not necessarily in the same way throughout Christian history. However, we are also told that in the last days many will fall away and follow after false teachers. (2 Pet 2:1-3) We should expect this and never lose heart or confidence. God's plans and God's promises will all come to fruition.

Acts 3:1-11

1 Now Peter and John went up together to the temple at the hour of prayer, the ninth hour. 2 And a certain man lame from his mother's womb was carried, whom they laid daily at the gate of the temple which is called Beautiful, to ask alms from those who entered the temple; 3 who, seeing Peter and John about to go into the temple, asked for alms. 4 And fixing his eyes on him, with John, Peter said, "Look at us." 5 So he gave them his attention, expecting to receive something from them. 6 Then Peter said, "Silver and gold I do not have, but what I do have I give you: In the name of Jesus Christ of Nazareth, rise up and walk." 7 And he took him by the right hand and lifted him up, and immediately his feet and ankle bones received strength. 8 So he, leaping up, stood and walked and entered the temple with them--walking, leaping, and praising God. 9 And all the people saw him walking and praising God. 10 Then they knew that it was he who sat begging alms at the Beautiful Gate of the temple; and they were filled with wonder and amazement at what had happened to him. 11 Now as the lame man who was healed held on to Peter and John, all the people ran together to them in the porch which is called Solomon's, greatly amazed.

In these verses we have a moving story of the first sign or wonder carried out by Jesus through the agency of the Apostles Peter and John. They had been close friends for a long time since their work together in a Galilean fishing business.

For one thing, we learn that they went to the temple to pray. There were three statutory times for daily prayer in the life of loyal Jews, and this one at three o'clock was the final one of the day. Prayer had ceased to become a mere observance and was now a vital joy. The reason for this is that Jesus had taught them how to pray all those months ago. Moreover, the indwelling Holy Spirit gave them the desire and the inspiration to pray. We are not told the content of these prayers but we can be sure that they began with praise, "Hallowed be Your name!"(Luke 11: 2) Do we have a desire and the inspiration to pray, just like these apostles?

For another thing, we learn that the poor expect help, including financial help from Christians. This poor crippled man put out his hand, to expect a small contribution. Christians down the centuries have so often fulfilled a duty to help in one way or another. Peter and John may have had a few coins on them, but they had little if any wealth, and certainly no silver or gold. We should note that they did not exploit their position as apostles to accumulate personal wealth.

We also note that this man showed no faith that he could be healed. He displayed no sign of repentance. As far as we know he had expressed no previous interest in Jesus. And yet, Peter spoke to him in that most powerful of names, "In the name of Jesus of Nazareth, rise up and walk." (v 6) The man was given a hand and he leapt to his feet. "The lame shall leap like a deer." (Isa. 35:6)

Our faith may be weak and faltering. At first, we may not understand the terrible nature of sin and our need of repentance. We may have a mere passing knowledge of Jesus but still we can be given a helping hand in the name of Jesus and be lifted up to praise Him. Many may remain uninterested for the whole of their lives, but no one is too far gone to become believer or a declarer of praise.

We also need to remember that when anyone becomes a Christian, Jesus Himself is filled with rejoicing. (Luke 10: 21).

Finally, we see that the healed man clung to Peter and John. In the same way we should cling to the apostles' doctrine as described in the Bible. We need also to cling to Christ because He has given us a reassuring promise that none can snatch us out of His Father's hand. (John 10: 29).

Acts 3:11-26

11 Now as the lame man who was healed held on to Peter and John, all the people ran together to them in the porch which is called Solomon's, greatly amazed. **12** So when Peter saw it, he responded to the people: "Men of Israel, why do you marvel at this? Or why look so intently at us, as though by our own power or godliness we had made this man walk? **13** The God of Abraham, Isaac, and Jacob, the God of our fathers, glorified His Servant Jesus, whom you delivered up and denied in the presence of Pilate, when he was determined to let Him go. **14** But you denied the Holy One and the Just, and asked for a murderer to be granted to you, **15** and killed the Prince of life, whom God raised from the dead, of which we are witnesses. **16** And His name, through faith in His name, has made this man strong, whom you see and know. Yes, the faith which comes through Him has given him this perfect soundness in the presence of you all. **17** Yet now, brethren, I know that you did it in ignorance, as did also your rulers. **18** But those things which God foretold by the mouth of all His prophets, that the Christ would suffer, He has thus fulfilled. **19** Repent therefore and be converted, that your sins may be blotted out, so that times of refreshing may come from the presence of the Lord, **20** and that He may send Jesus Christ, who was preached to you before, **21** whom heaven must receive until the times of restoration of all things, which God has spoken by the mouth of all His holy prophets since the world began. **22** For Moses truly said to the fathers, 'The Lord your God will raise up for you a Prophet like me from your brethren. Him you shall hear in all things, whatever He says to you. **23** And it shall be that every soul who will not hear that Prophet shall be utterly destroyed from among the people.' **24** Yes, and all the prophets, from Samuel and those who follow, as many as have spoken, have also foretold these days. **25** You are sons of the prophets, and of the covenant which God made with our fathers, saying to Abraham, 'And in your seed all the families of the earth shall be blessed.' **26** To you first, God, having raised up His Servant Jesus, sent Him to bless you, in turning away every one of you from your iniquities.

We have in front of us Peter's second sermon as recorded in Acts. Both sermons are explanations of dramatic events. The first was on the day of Pentecost when the disciples spoke in foreign languages. The second is an explanation of a wonderful miraculous healing of a man who was born lame. The fact that he was born lame emphasizes the lack of the possibility that it was a mere psychological change. In the same way there is on record in John's Gospel a miracle or sign when Jesus healed a man who was born blind.

The sermon contains a number of themes, which we should mark well.

The first is that both Peter and John shifted the praise from themselves to God in no uncertain terms. They insisted that it was the "God of our fathers" and Jesus who had done this miracle. (v 12-13) It is a natural wish to take praise but we need to give God the glory for what He has done in all our lives. We need to state this to others and feel it in our hearts. We cannot hide our thoughts and intentions from God. He knows all about us. "He knows the secrets of the heart." (Psa. 44:21)

The second theme is about Jesus who is given a messianic divine title, "the Holy one and the Just". Peter shows great courage when he casts the blame on the people of Jerusalem for disowning and killing their Messiah. "The Prince of life." (v 15) Not only that, the crowd, only a few weeks previously, wanted a murderer to go free!

Then Peter delivered the masterstroke. God raised Jesus to life and we are witnesses. Their authority was demonstrated and authenticated by the miracle that had taken place. Peter and John had to be heard.

The next theme was the good news. It demonstrated God's most precious love for His people. The residents of Jerusalem did what they did in ignorance, but paradoxically the death of Jesus and His resurrection was part of God's plan. God had brought salvation to His people out what was an initial, apparently hopeless situation. Later, the Apostle Paul asserted that his behaviour before he was a Christian was carried out in ignorance and unbelief. (1 Tim 1:13) The sad thing is that many are still quite happy to remain in ignorance. There is none so blind as those that won't see!

The marvellous thing is that although these people and indeed all of us are under judgement, God has given us a way of repentance so that we can be forgiven and come into a wonderful relationship with the Lord Jesus. His desire is to bless. (v 20)

The final theme is that Peter reinforced his argument by an appeal to the Hebrew Scriptures, and that Jesus is that prophet, that Messiah, who had been foretold to Abraham and by Moses, Samuel and David:

Moses said, "The Lord your God will raise up for you a Prophet like me from your midst, from your brethren. Him you shall hear. (Deuteronomy 18:15) And it shall be that every soul who will not hear that Prophet shall be utterly destroyed from among the people". (v 23)

Believers should always have in mind the awesome nature and judgement of God, together with the love, grace, kindness, and patience of God our Father.

Acts 4:1-22

1 Now as they spoke to the people, the priests, the captain of the temple, and the Sadducees came upon them, 2 being greatly disturbed that they taught the people and preached in Jesus the resurrection from the dead. 3 And they laid hands on them, and put them in custody until the next day, for it was already evening. 4 However, many of those who heard the word believed; and the number of the men came to be about five thousand. 5 And it came to pass, on the next day, that their rulers, elders, and scribes, 6 as well as Annas the high priest, Caiaphas, John, and Alexander, and as many as were of the family of the high priest, were gathered together at Jerusalem. 7 And when they had set them in the midst, they asked, "By what power or by what name have you done this?" 8 Then Peter, filled with the Holy Spirit, said to them, "Rulers of the people and elders of Israel: 9 If we this day are judged for a good deed done to a helpless man, by what means he has been made well, 10 let it be known to you all, and to all the people of Israel, that by the name of Jesus Christ of Nazareth, whom you crucified, whom God raised from the dead, by Him this man stands here before you whole. 11 This is the 'stone which was rejected by you builders, which has become the chief cornerstone.' 12 Nor is there salvation in any other, for there is no other name under heaven given among men by which we must be saved." 13 Now when they saw the boldness of Peter and John, and perceived that they were uneducated and untrained men, they marveled. And they realized that they had been with Jesus. 14 And seeing the man who had been healed standing with them, they could say nothing against it. 15 But when they had commanded them to go aside out of the council, they conferred among themselves, 16 saying, "What shall we do to these men? For, indeed, that a notable miracle has been done through them is evident to all who dwell in Jerusalem, and we cannot deny it. 17 But so that it spreads no further among the people, let us severely threaten them, that from now on they speak to no man in this name." 18 And they called them and commanded them not to speak at all nor teach in the name of Jesus. 19 But Peter and John answered and said to them, "Whether it is right in the sight of God to listen to you more than to God, you judge. 20 For we cannot but speak the things which we have seen and heard." 21 So when they had further threatened them, they let them go, finding no way of punishing them, because of the people, since they all glorified God for what had been done. 22 For the man was over forty years old on whom this miracle of healing had been performed.

After a few astonishing weeks of the early church in action, with demonstrations of worship, teaching, great joy and love, we move to the first opposition, hatred and persecution It was the commencement of persecution that has continued in various forms and intensity until the present day. The world is glad to see and receive, and may even admire social and charitable work by the church, but when preachers and Christians in general talk about sin, righteousness and judgement, then the mood and tone changes.

Until that time, the Sadducees and priests were opponents of Jesus and had delivered Jesus to the Romans to be crucified. They were faced with the fact that Christ now had yet another five thousand male followers, let alone women and children. They hauled Peter and John before the Sanhedrin, the seventy-strong group of ruling Jews. Peter and John had, at last, an opportunity to share the gospel with this most exclusive class.

We have in the behaviour and words of Peter and John a number of lessons

Firstly, they remained peaceful and respectful under this most severe of judicial pressure. They followed the example of their master. Peter would write years later:

" For to this you were called, because Christ also suffered for us, leaving us an example, that you should follow His steps: "Who committed no sin, Nor was deceit found in His mouth"; who, when He was reviled, did not revile in return; when He suffered, He did not threaten, but committed Himself to Him who judges righteously; who Himself bore our sins in His own body on the tree, that we, having died to sins, might live for righteousness--by whose stripes you were healed. (1 Pet. 2:21-24)

Secondly, we read that Peter was filled with the Holy Spirit. This was a special infilling that God can give to those facing trouble for Him.

Jesus promises that when we are brought before courts we should not worry, and He will give us the words to say. (Luke 21:12-19) We often think that we would wilt under suffering and persecution, but God draws even closer to us in these circumstances to give both strength and courage.

Thirdly, Peter and John were mocked as being unlearned and not having attended the right school. They were tradesmen. John Bunyan, the great seventeenth century writer and preacher, Evan Roberts of the Welsh revival, and Gladys Aylward who went to China were all in this category, but they were used wonderfully by God. Degrees and education are important, but the most important qualifications are, firstly, to be taught by Christ through His word, and, secondly, to be called by God. The critics of the Apostles stated that these men had been with Jesus. May it be said of all who call themselves believers, "They have been with Jesus."

Fourthly, although Peter and John were respectful, they still spoke with great courage. They could have toned down their message to suit their hearers, or said that they would modify their preaching, but no! Peter emphasized that the poor beggar at the beautiful gate was miraculously and by implication not magically healed. The power was that of Jesus of Nazareth whom they had crucified! Peter quoted scripture again and then delivered the climax, which we should always carry with us. "Nor is there salvation in any other, for there is no other name under heaven given among men by which we must be saved." (v12) Jesus stated clearly that no one could come to the Father but by Him. (John 14:6) The hymn writer put it aptly when he wrote, "In Christ alone my hope is found." So it is not by mere human effort or other belief system that we can approach God or gain heaven or any salvation. The gospel is inclusive in that none is outside its remit, but exclusive in that faith in Jesus is the only way. Certain religious people have done the world the greatest of disservice when they have taught that there are many paths to God. There is one way and it is a narrow path, (Matt 7: 13) and it begins at the cross.

Finally, the Sanhedrin were totally unmoved. They had to admit that a miracle had happened, but their options were limited, because the thousands of new believers were still present in Jerusalem. So they used threatening aggressive language, coupled with a warning and then let them go. Even though they accepted that a miracle to a forty-year old man had taken place, they still remained in aggressive unbelief. Peter and John had left their fishing business to follow Christ but these men of power and wealth were prepared to relinquish and modify nothing. We all have to adjust our lives and lifestyles to follow Christ, but nearly all with much wealth and power would rather hang on to their privileges rather than follow the way of Jesus. Thankfully, there are the few, "With God all things are possible." (Matt 19: 26)

Acts 4:23-31

23 And being let go, they went to their own companions and reported all that the chief priests and elders had said to them. **24** So when they heard that, they raised their voice to God with one accord and said: "Lord, You are God, who made heaven and earth and the sea, and all that is in them, **25** who by the mouth of Your servant David have said: 'Why did the nations rage, And the people plot vain things? **26** The kings of the earth took their stand, And the rulers were gathered together Against the Lord and against His Christ.' **27** "For truly against Your holy Servant Jesus, whom You anointed, both Herod and Pontius Pilate, with the Gentiles and the people of Israel, were gathered together **28** to do whatever Your hand and Your purpose determined before to be done. **29** Now, Lord, look on their threats, and grant to Your servants that with all boldness they may speak Your word, **30** by stretching out Your hand to heal, and that signs and wonders may be done through the name of Your holy Servant Jesus." **31** And when they had prayed, the place where they were assembled together was shaken; and they were all filled with the Holy Spirit, and they spoke the word of God with boldness.

We now move on to the first prayer meeting of the growing church recorded in Acts. Peter and John reported back to the fellowship all that had happened. Instead of being shocked and frightened, they were elated and full of praise to God. They were reassured in their prayer that they should expect opposition and that this was in keeping with what had been foretold in the Scriptures.

We learn in the first place the importance of the prayer meeting. It is sad that the weekly prayer meeting is often only attended by a comparative few. We all have busy lives and we all have other commitments, but the prayer meeting should be a top priority. A strong church may not be strong in numbers but by definition is strong in prayer. A prayerful church can shake the world. In the passage here, the house where they met, literally did shake.

We note in the second place that they were full of praise to God.

We so often come to Him with a catalogue of demands that we forget to note all that God has done and is doing. In the process of prayer, it is often good to quote God's word. And from that position move on to make known our requests:

Be anxious for nothing, but in everything by prayer and supplication, with thanksgiving, let your requests be made known to God; and the peace of God, which surpasses all understanding, will guard your hearts and minds through Christ Jesus. (Phil 4: 6-7)

In the third place, they prayed for boldness. Many Christians, like Timothy, are sensitive and timid by nature. (2 Tim 1: 7) Christians, moved by the Holy Spirit, can become bold in witness. We need to remember that Timothy became courageous in his faith and we do know that at one point was put in prison. (Heb.13: 23) We are so often scared of saying the wrong thing that we say nothing. Ask God to help you choose the right situation, and then the right words.

Acts 4:32-37

32 Now the multitude of those who believed were of one heart and one soul; neither did anyone say that any of the things he possessed was his own, but they had all things in common. **33** And with great power the apostles gave witness to the resurrection of the Lord Jesus. And great grace was upon them all. **34** Nor was there anyone among them who lacked; for all who were possessors of lands or houses sold them, and brought the proceeds of the things that were sold, **35** and laid them at the apostles' feet; and they distributed to each as anyone had need. **36** And Joses, who was also named Barnabas by the apostles (which is translated Son of Encouragement), a Levite of the country of Cyprus, **37** having land, sold it, and brought the money and laid it at the apostles' feet.

In this short passage we have a sublime second picture of the early church. Once again, there is a moving description of Christian love and fellowship. There is nothing quite like it in the whole world. The centre is the Lord Jesus and the powerful apostolic testimony to the resurrection. There were thousands of Jews from around the world who were still in Jerusalem and these learning believers required food and shelter. The response was massive as hearts opened up to the needs of others. They shared everything they had. Some were even prepared to sell their houses and property, and put the proceeds at the apostles' feet. This picture of the first weeks of the early church is not repeated elsewhere in Acts or the epistles. Nevertheless, may God grant to all believers with means, generous spirits. No one was more generous than Jesus, who gave "His life as a ransom for many". (Mark 10: 45) There are few people who are more 'sad' than mean-spirited, small-minded, stunted Christians.

At the end of this chapter we are introduced to Joseph Barnabas. He was a Levite, that is, he was of a priestly family. Many of the Sanhedrin were priests and were well-to-do, just as Barnabas was. The difference was that he believed in Jesus and the resurrection, they refused. He gave his life to Jesus and sold his field in order to place money at the Apostles' feet and invest in the Kingdom of God. They would not and did not. The contrast that Luke describes in this chapter appears to be intentional.

Barnabas was a godly man and a 'people person'. He was known for the help and encouragement he gave to others, most notably, as we shall see later, to Saul of Tarsus and John Mark. Happy is the fellowship that contains people like Barnabas. We frequently need to give greater encouragement than we do. Leaders in a church need to encourage their church members, and develop any gifts they may have. Furthermore, those who teach God's Word and those who labour for the gospel need words and demonstrations of encouragement. When did we last give words of encouragement?

Acts 5:1-11

1 But a certain man named Ananias, with Sapphira his wife, sold a possession. **2** And he kept back part of the proceeds, his wife also being aware of it, and brought a certain part and laid it at the apostles' feet. **3** But Peter said, "Ananias, why has Satan filled your heart to lie to the Holy Spirit and keep back part of the price of the land for yourself? **4** While it remained, was it not your own? And after it was sold, was it not in your own control? Why have you conceived this thing in your heart? You have not lied to men but to God." **5** Then Ananias, hearing these words, fell down and breathed his last. So great fear came upon all those who heard these things. **6** And the young men arose and wrapped him up, carried him out, and buried him. **7** Now it was about three hours later when his wife came in, not knowing what had happened. **8** And Peter answered her, "Tell me whether you sold the land for so much?" She said, "Yes, for so much." **9** Then Peter said to her, "How is it that you have agreed together to test the Spirit of the Lord? Look, the feet of those who have buried your husband are at the door, and they will carry you out." **10** Then immediately she fell down at his feet and breathed her last. And the young men came in and found her dead, and carrying her out, buried her by her husband. **11** So great fear came upon all the church and upon all who heard these things.

After the first external threat to the young church the story proceeds to an internal threat, more subtle, yet potentially more devastating. Following the example of Barnabas, Ananias and Sapphira were a couple who no doubt wished to impress the church and the apostles by a huge donation, perhaps the largest to date. In doing so, they would bask in the acclaim that they anticipated would come to them. Nevertheless, they lied. They tried to give the impression that all the money from a sale of property was going to the church and those in need. In fact, they kept a large portion for themselves. They received swift and powerful judgement.

There are some issues which this story highlights.

The first issue is that those who lie to God, particularly with reference to the fellowship, are committing a great offence to God. If we think that we can deceive God, we are putting ourselves on a par with God. God knows all about us. Jesus said to the church in Thyatira that it is He who "searches hearts and minds". (Rev 2:23) "Man looks at the outward appearance, but the Lord looks at the heart." (1 Sam 16:7) Whatever appearance we give to the world, the church, or even our family and best friends, we cannot fool God! God is not mocked. (Gal 6:7)

The second issue is that there are many instances throughout the Bible where people who sin against God are given time and many chances to repent. In Jesus' letters to the churches He talks about coming judgement, but we also have a gracious picture of Jesus knocking patiently at the door of the human heart. (Rev 3:20)

After deciding to deceive the Apostles, both Ananias and Sapphira were struck dead in front of the whole church; first Ananias and then his wife, three hours later. A similar thing happened to Achan in the book of Joshua, (Joshua 7: 1- 26) and before that to the sons of Aaron. (Lev 10: 1-2) We must not treat the commands of God lightly. There are some who may say that God is unfair, but we accept that there should be punishment of paedophiles and fraudsters in the financial industry. If our anger is just in those instances, we need to accept that God's wrath is also just and far more so. We cannot have perfect love without perfect holiness. "You are of purer eyes than to behold evil, And cannot look on wickedness." (Hab. 1:13)

The German poet and journalist Heinriche Heine supposedly gave this answer when a priest asked him on his deathbed if he thought God would forgive his sin. "Of course God will forgive me - that's His job." Heine's defiant complacency could not be more wrong!

The third issue that arises here is somewhat speculative. Were this husband and wife true believers, were they really Christians? I tend to think that they were. If indeed they were, then we are left with the solemn conclusion, that God may bring severe judgement on His people in this world, and even death, although they are ultimately saved:

For the time has come for judgment to begin at the house of God; and if it begins with us first, what will be the end of those who do not obey the gospel of God? (1 Pet. 4:17)

Judgement on members of the church of God was described by Paul in relation to the Lord's Supper. He states:

For he who eats and drinks in an unworthy manner eats and drinks judgment to himself, not discerning the Lord's body. For this reason many are weak and sick among you, and many sleep (1 Cor. 11: 29-30)

At this critical moment in the young church's history, no wonder awe and fear seized the whole church and all who heard about these events. (v 11)

Acts 5:12-28

12 And through the hands of the apostles many signs and wonders were done among the people. And they were all with one accord in Solomon's Porch. **13** Yet none of the rest dared join them, but the people esteemed them highly. **14** And believers were increasingly added to the Lord, multitudes of both men and women, **15** so that they brought the sick out into the streets and laid them on beds and couches, that at least the shadow of Peter passing by might fall on some of them. **16** Also a multitude gathered from the surrounding cities to Jerusalem, bringing sick people and those who were tormented by unclean spirits, and they were all healed. **17** Then the high priest rose up, and all those who were with him (which is the sect of the Sadducees), and they were filled with indignation, **18** and laid their hands on the apostles and put them in the common prison. **19** But at night an angel of the Lord opened the prison doors and brought them out, and said, **20** "Go, stand in the temple and speak to the people all the words of this life." **21** And when they heard that, they entered the temple early in the morning and taught. But the high priest and those with him came and called the council together, with all the elders of the children of Israel, and sent to the prison to have them brought. **22** But when the officers came and did not find them in the prison, they returned and reported, **23** saying, "Indeed we found the prison shut securely, and the guards standing outside before the doors; but when we opened them, we found no one inside!" **24** Now when the high priest, the captain of the temple, and the chief priests heard these things, they wondered what the outcome would be. **25** So one came and told them, saying, "Look, the men whom you put in prison are standing in the temple and teaching the people!" **26** Then the captain went with the officers and brought them without violence, for they feared the people, lest they should be stoned. **27** And when they had brought them, they set them before the council. And the high priest asked them, **28** saying, "Did we not strictly command you not to teach in this name? And look, you have filled Jerusalem with your doctrine, and intend to bring this Man's blood on us!

After the deaths of Ananias and Sapphira, the church advanced. It seemed to dominate the life of Jerusalem and also surrounding towns. We note for one thing, the gracious blessing and gentleness in God's dealing with His people. People were healed and lives brought into the kingdom of God. It was one of those foretastes of future glory when there will be no more sickness, no more tears and no more death. (Rev 21: 4) We should ask ourselves, "Is this our expectation?" Pray that this vision may become part of the fabric of your life.

For another thing we see the inevitable opposition by the high priest and the Sadducees towards the progress of the true gospel. Then as now, it was done out of jealousy and a refusal to admit that they too were sinners and needed a Saviour. Persecution can so often come from the respectable religious.

Nevertheless, in spite of warnings, they continued to preach and teach with confidence and boldness. The miraculous release from prison of the apostles and their continuing advancement out-manoeuvred the authorities.

One of the most difficult places to witness is at work when we are in a high pressure, high expectation team, working for a highly qualified, able, yet unbelieving boss. God knows all about it, He knows that we have to work; He knows that the job is demanding. God is on our side, and at our side. The Apostle Paul gave sound advice in a very different situation, at a time when there was the burden of slavery:

Bondservants, be obedient to those who are your masters according to the flesh, with fear and trembling, in sincerity of heart, as to Christ; not with eyeservice, as men-pleasers, but as bondservants of Christ, doing the will of God from the heart. (Eph. 6:5-6)

Finally, the members of the Sanhedrin were worried that they might be made guilty of Jesus' blood.(v 28) The fact is, they were guilty of His blood. Moreover, the whole world stands guilty and under judgement. (Ro 3:19) We are all guilty, but Jesus' blood cleanses us from all sin; (1 John 1:7).What grace, what forgiveness, what love! Sadly, the rulers in Jerusalem had no desire at all to admit to any kind of wrong and avail themselves of God's forgiveness.

Acts 5:29-42

29 But Peter and the other apostles answered and said: "We ought to obey God rather than men. **30** The God of our fathers raised up Jesus whom you murdered by hanging on a tree. **31** Him God has exalted to His right hand to be Prince and Savior, to give repentance to Israel and forgiveness of sins. **32** And we are His witnesses to these things, and so also is the Holy Spirit whom God has given to those who obey Him." **33** When they heard this, they were furious and plotted to kill them. **34** Then one in the council stood up, a Pharisee named Gamaliel, a teacher of the law held in respect by all the people, and commanded them to put the apostles outside for a little while. **35** And he said to them: "Men of Israel, take heed to yourselves what you intend to do regarding these men. **36** For some time ago Theudas rose up, claiming to be somebody. A number of men, about four hundred, joined him. He was slain, and all who obeyed him were scattered and came to nothing. **37** After this man, Judas of Galilee rose up in the days of the census, and drew away many people after him. He also perished, and all who obeyed him were dispersed. **38** And now I say to you, keep away from these men and let them alone; for if this plan or this work is of men, it will come to nothing; **39** but if it is of God, you cannot overthrow it--lest you even be found to fight against God." **40** And they agreed with him, and when they had called for the apostles and beaten them, they commanded that they should not speak in the name of Jesus, and let them go. **41** So they departed from the presence of the council, rejoicing that they were counted worthy to suffer shame for His name. **42** And daily in the temple, and in every house, they did not cease teaching and preaching Jesus as the Christ.

From this passage we can note a number of topics.

Firstly, Peter and the apostles emphasized that they must obey God rather than men. We so often have to obey men, in and out of the workplace. It is right to obey laws and rules. It is self evident that without laws and rules, countries and societies could not function:

Remind them to be subject to rulers and authorities, to obey, to be ready for every good work, to speak evil of no one, to be peaceable, gentle, showing all humility to all men. (Titus 3:1-2)

However, when laws, rules and authorities come into conflict with God's ways, we should rather obey God. Compromise can be and often is a virtue. However, a church that compromises over vital Christian teaching leads to a weak and even a corrupt church.

Secondly, we are introduced to the top intellectual in Israel, Gamaliel. His hotheaded colleagues called for the death penalty against the Apostles. He had a different view. He even expressed the possibility that this new movement could be of God. After some historical examples, he indicated that the influence of the 'Jesus people' might just slowly wilt away. Although he warned that no-one could resist God, there is no evidence that he ever became a believer. Perhaps he was prevented by his intellectual pride. We are fortunate that there are judges, leaders in industry and the professions, who are just like Gamaliel, and able to give wise counsel, but it is even sadder that many of these people are unable or unwilling to give themselves to Christ.

Finally, Gamaliel may have advised against the death penalty, but he did not prevent a flogging. This is the first physical punishment in the long history of persecution against Christians. Flogging was a cruel and violent punishment. It consisted of thirty-nine strikes with the lash that ripped both skin and muscle. Paul also suffered this terrible treatment. "Five times I received from the Jews the forty stripes minus one." (2 Cor. 11:24)

Many would have been broken by the pain and disgrace. A few months before, the disciples fled at the arrest of Jesus but these courageous men rejoiced because they were found worthy to suffer for the Name.

Peter himself later wrote:

But rejoice to the extent that you partake of Christ's sufferings, that when His glory is revealed, you may also be glad with exceeding joy. (1 Pet. 4:13)

Many in various parts of the world at this very moment are undergoing trials and terrible persecution. We need to remember them in our prayers.

Acts 6:1-7

1 Now in those days, when the number of the disciples was multiplying, there arose a complaint against the Hebrews by the Hellenists, because their widows were neglected in the daily distribution. 2 Then the twelve summoned the multitude of the disciples and said, "It is not desirable that we should leave the word of God and serve tables. 3 Therefore, brethren, seek out from among you seven men of good reputation, full of the Holy Spirit and wisdom, whom we may appoint over this business; 4 but we will give ourselves continually to prayer and to the ministry of the word." 5 And the saying pleased the whole multitude. And they chose Stephen, a man full of faith and the Holy Spirit, and Philip, Prochorus, Nicanor, Timon, Parmenas, and Nicolas, a proselyte from Antioch, 6 whom they set before the apostles; and when they had prayed, they laid hands on them. 7 Then the word of God spread, and the number of the disciples multiplied greatly in Jerusalem, and a great many of the priests were obedient to the faith.

The narrative moves onto another challenge that faced the young church. The growth of any movement leads to the necessity of management and administration. Poor administration leads to frustration. Good administration leads to enabling. This passage teaches some helpful lessons.

The first lesson is that proper comment and criticism is generally very helpful. When given in good faith, church leaders need to come to wise decisions and act promptly.

There were no social services in those days and the fellowship took upon itself the role of provision for those in need. Widows were often without any means of support and the Grecian Jews felt that there was an unequal distribution. Such a complaint leads us to the second lesson.

Complaints can develop into what the old translations referred to as 'murmuring'. Few things can be more injurious to a church than harmful gossip and constant grim dissatisfaction. The Israelites murmured against Moses and the Lord whilst in the wilderness. This led to a wandering that lasted forty years. It is a wise saying "If we have nothing useful to say, then don't say it."

The third lesson is that the apostles recognised the priority and importance of teaching. They did not want to get bogged down in administration. That is a most important lesson for today's Christian teachers, and also the members of churches. Many a gifted ministry has been stunted by an overwhelming administrative burden.

The fourth lesson is the need for wise choices in the making of appointments. It was crucial that they got it right when it came to food distribution. The appointment of the first deacons showed much wisdom. It addressed the complaint by appointing deacons who had Greek names. This would have reassured the Grecian Jewish widows. Most importantly, they had to be men full of the Holy Spirit, with all the kindness and patience that such a gifting would demonstrate. Nowhere in the New Testament did anyone say, "I am full of the Holy Spirit." It was others who could see what was happening. The apostles showed their appreciation and the importance of this ministry by prayer, and the laying on of hands.

Finally, the resolution of this grievance led to further growth, and this time, priests became obedient to the faith. Even those who are most critical of the faith can change.

Acts 6:8-15

8 And Stephen, full of faith and power, did great wonders and signs among the people. **9** Then there arose some from what is called the Synagogue of the Freedmen (Cyrenians, Alexandrians, and those from Cilicia and Asia), disputing with Stephen. **10** And they were not able to resist the wisdom and the Spirit by which he spoke. **11** Then they secretly induced men to say, "We have heard him speak blasphemous words against Moses and God." **12** And they stirred up the people, the elders, and the scribes; and they came upon him, seized him, and brought him to the council. **13** They also set up false witnesses who said, "This man does not cease to speak blasphemous words against this holy place and the law; **14** for we have heard him say that this Jesus of Nazareth will destroy this place and change the customs which Moses delivered to us." **15** And all who sat in the council, looking steadfastly at him, saw his face as the face of an angel.

Stephen has already been introduced as the first mentioned amongst the deacons, and full of the Holy Spirit. He is now introduced as a man full of grace and power. "He did great wonders and signs among the people." (v 8) The church was moving from the local Jews to those who were from the Diaspora. There were numerous synagogues in Jerusalem and Stephen went to speak in those whose members were from North Africa, and parts we would now call Turkey. One of the areas included the city of Tarsus. It may have been that Stephen went head to head with none other than Saul of Tarsus, but even the highly intelligent unconverted Saul was "not able to resist the wisdom and the Spirit by which he spoke." (v 10)

There are a few points here in these verses to give us instruction.

For one thing, the people of God are truly blessed when the really gifted, those with natural and spiritual gifts are encouraged in their use. We need both men and women who are able to contend earnestly for the faith. There is much opposition in the world today, both secular and religious. We should pray for bold apologists to speak up for the gospel.

For another thing, we can expect opponents of the gospel to stir up trouble. They may misread, misquote and misunderstand. In some parts of the world they may even bring believers before a court. Nevertheless, the accusations here did contain some validity. Stephen could see quite clearly that Jesus' death on the cross had superseded all temple sacrifices. Jesus Himself was the full, perfect and sufficient sacrifice for sin. The gospel made many parts of the law, no longer binding, and therefore, no longer applicable. The indwelling Spirit made the idea that the Jerusalem temple was the place where God dwell obsolete.

Finally, we note that Stephen's face was like that of an angel. Stephen seemed to know what the outcome of the trial would be. He knew that he would be found guilty. He knew that the penalty would be death by stoning. I have known Christians during their final days to have had radiant faces. It is as if they have had a glimpse of heaven. The clamour of this world becomes dimmer as the music of heaven becomes sweeter, louder and clearer. Such was the nature of this gifted, godly powerful servant of the Lord.

Acts 7:1-53

1 Then the high priest said, "Are these things so?" 2 And he said, "Brethren and fathers, listen: The God of glory appeared to our father Abraham when he was in Mesopotamia, before he dwelt in Haran, 3 and said to him, 'Get out of your country and from your relatives, and come to a land that I will show you.' 4 Then he came out of the land of the Chaldeans and dwelt in Haran. And from there, when his father was dead, He moved him to this land in which you now dwell. 5 And God gave him no inheritance in it, not even enough to set his foot on. But even when Abraham had no child, He promised to give it to him for a possession, and to his descendants after him. 6 But God spoke in this way: that his descendants would dwell in a foreign land, and that they would bring them into bondage and oppress them four hundred years. 7 'And the nation to whom they will be in bondage I will judge,' said God, 'and after that they shall come out and serve Me in this place.' 8 Then He gave him the covenant of circumcision; and so Abraham begot Isaac and circumcised him on the eighth day; and Isaac begot Jacob, and Jacob begot the twelve patriarchs. 9 "And the patriarchs, becoming envious, sold Joseph into Egypt. But God was with him 10 and delivered him out of all his troubles, and gave him favor and wisdom in the presence of Pharaoh, king of Egypt; and he made him governor over Egypt and all his house. 11 Now a famine and great trouble came over all the land of Egypt and Canaan, and our fathers found no sustenance. 12 But when Jacob heard that there was grain in Egypt, he sent out our fathers first. 13 And the second time Joseph was made known to his brothers, and Joseph's family became known to the Pharaoh. 14 Then Joseph sent and called his father Jacob and all his relatives to him, seventy-five people. 15 So Jacob went down to Egypt; and he died, he and our fathers. 16 And they were carried back to Shechem and laid in the tomb that Abraham bought for a sum of money from the sons of Hamor, the father of Shechem. 17 "But when the time of the promise drew near which God had sworn to Abraham, the people grew and multiplied in Egypt 18 till another king arose who did not know Joseph. 19 This man dealt treacherously with our people, and oppressed our forefathers, making them expose their babies, so that they might not live. 20 At this time Moses was born, and was well pleasing to God; and he was brought up in his father's house for three months. 21 But when he was set out, Pharaoh's daughter took him away and brought him up as her own son. 22 And Moses was learned in

all the wisdom of the Egyptians, and was mighty in words and deeds. **23** Now when he was forty years old, it came into his heart to visit his brethren, the children of Israel. **24** And seeing one of them suffer wrong, he defended and avenged him who was oppressed, and struck down the Egyptian. **25** For he supposed that his brethren would have understood that God would deliver them by his hand, but they did not understand. **26** And the next day he appeared to two of them as they were fighting, and tried to reconcile them, saying, 'Men, you are brethren; why do you wrong one another?' **27** But he who did his neighbor wrong pushed him away, saying, 'Who made you a ruler and a judge over us? **28** Do you want to kill me as you did the Egyptian yesterday?' **29** Then, at this saying, Moses fled and became a dweller in the land of Midian, where he had two sons. **30** And when forty years had passed, an Angel of the Lord appeared to him in a flame of fire in a bush, in the wilderness of Mount Sinai. **31** When Moses saw it, he marveled at the sight; and as he drew near to observe, the voice of the Lord came to him, **32** saying, 'I am the God of your fathers--the God of Abraham, the God of Isaac, and the God of Jacob.' And Moses trembled and dared not look. **33** 'Then the Lord said to him, "Take your sandals off your feet, for the place where you stand is holy ground. **34** I have surely seen the oppression of my people who are in Egypt; I have heard their groaning and have come down to deliver them. And now come, I will send you to Egypt." ' **35** This Moses whom they rejected, saying, 'Who made you a ruler and a judge?' is the one God sent to be a ruler and a deliverer by the hand of the Angel who appeared to him in the bush. **36** He brought them out, after he had shown wonders and signs in the land of Egypt, and in the Red Sea, and in the wilderness forty years. **37** "This is that Moses who said to the children of Israel, 'The Lord your God will raise up for you a Prophet like me from your brethren. Him you shall hear.' **38** This is he who was in the congregation in the wilderness with the Angel who spoke to him on Mount Sinai, and with our fathers, the one who received the living oracles to give to us, **39** whom our fathers would not obey, but rejected. And in their hearts they turned back to Egypt, **40** saying to Aaron, 'Make us gods to go before us; as for this Moses who brought us out of the land of Egypt, we do not know what has become of him.' **41** And they made a calf in those days, offered sacrifices to the idol, and rejoiced in the works of their own hands. **42** Then God turned and gave them up to worship the host of heaven, as it is written in the book of the Prophets: 'Did you offer Me slaughtered animals and sacrifices during forty years in the wilderness, O house of Israel? **43** You also took up the tabernacle of Moloch, And the star of your god Remphan, Images which you made to worship; And I will carry you away beyond Babylon.' **44** "Our fathers had the tabernacle of witness in the wilderness, as He appointed, instructing Moses to make it according to the pattern that he had seen, **45** which our fathers, having received it in turn, also brought with Joshua into the land possessed by the Gentiles, whom God drove out before the face of our fathers until the days of David, **46** who found favor before God and asked to find a dwelling for the God of Jacob. **47** But Solomon built Him a house. **48** However, the Most High does not dwell in temples made with hands, as the prophet says: **49** 'Heaven is My throne, And earth is My footstool. What house will you build for Me? says the Lord, Or what is the place of My rest? **50** Has My hand not made all these things?' **51** "You stiffnecked and uncircumcised in heart and ears! You always resist the Holy Spirit; as your fathers did, so do you. **52** Which of the prophets did your fathers not persecute? And they killed those who foretold the coming of the Just One, of whom you now have become the betrayers and murderers, **53** who have received the law by the direction of angels and have not kept it."

We observe from the length of this passage the importance that Luke and the Holy Spirit give to the last testimony of Stephen. We should read the passage and the history lesson it contains with great care. The crucial events of thousands of years of Jewish history are outlined here and Christians would be wise to familiarize themselves with them.

Stephen began to answer the issues of which the court accused him. They said that he blasphemed God and Moses, that he spoke against the temple and attempted to change the customs, which, they claimed, Moses had given down to them.

Stephen spoke respectfully, when he began, "Brethren and Fathers." (v 2) He started from where his hearers and he would agree. The accusation that he blasphemed God is countered immediately when he exclaimed, "The God of glory appeared to our Father Abraham." (v 2) Stephen believed in God! This title, "God of glory", appears only in the Psalms. (Ps. 29:3) Stephen then walked his way through Israel's history, and in doing so, drew his hearers' attention to various faithful men. We can mark a number of key subjects.

Firstly, we see what a great man of faith Abraham was. He was prepared to leave all the conveniences of his home city-state with all its idolatry in order to follow God's call. Those who come to Christ always have to set aside something in order to respond and be obedient to God. Sometimes we relinquish them with ease, sometimes with heart-searching and difficulty, but ultimately with gratitude.

Secondly, we mark that the plans of God can take centuries to come to pass. Abraham was told that his descendants would be enslaved for hundreds of years. It is not by accident that one of the fruits of the Spirit is patience.

Thirdly, we mark that the way of obedience can be a way of hardship. Abraham and his family did not possess the land where they lived. He clung on to God's promise.

Fourthly, and this is very important in the context of the trial, God's favoured servant, Joseph, was initially rejected by his brothers, the patriarchs of Israel. Furthermore, Moses was rejected by the Israelites at first after the "judicial" killing of an Egyptian, and later during their wanderings in the wilderness. The Israelites grumbled, wanted to return to Egypt, and wanted to go after other gods.

Fifthly, after reference to Joshua, Stephen began to arrive at the climax of his address. David and Solomon were key instruments in the construction of the temple. However, despite the importance of the temple, God, "does not live in temples made with hands". (v 48) Many 'church people' become so attached to their place of worship that they lose sight of the fact that we worship a transcendent God. God is more concerned with people and the gospel than He is with buildings. Tourists often refer to locations, such as Ayers Rock or certain exotic places and temples, as being 'spiritual'. Rather, it is people who are spiritual, people who employ their God-given gifts, believers who show the fruits of the Spirit, such as love joy and peace. (Gal. 5:22) These are the ones who are truly spiritual.

Finally, Stephen made his charge against his accusers. The Israelites were in the habit of rejecting Joseph, Moses, and the prophets whom they persecuted, and now they had rejected the Righteous One, whom they had murdered! It was not Stephen who had blasphemed God and Moses, but his accusers.

How crucial it is that those who call themselves Christian must not reject and persecute God's favoured individuals. In fact, Christians should not persecute anyone!

Acts 7:54-8:1

54 When they heard these things they were cut to the heart, and they gnashed at him with their teeth. **55** But he, being full of the Holy Spirit, gazed into heaven and saw the glory of God, and Jesus standing at the right hand of God, **56** and said, "Look! I see the heavens opened and the Son of Man standing at the right hand of God!" **57** Then they cried out with a loud voice, stopped their ears, and ran at him with one accord; **58** and they cast him out of the city and stoned him. And the witnesses laid down their clothes at the feet of a young man named Saul. **59** And they stoned Stephen as he was calling on God and saying, "Lord Jesus, receive my spirit." **60** Then he knelt down and cried out with a loud voice, "Lord, do not charge them with this sin." And when he had said this, he fell asleep. **1** Now Saul was consenting to his death. At that time a great persecution arose against the church which was at Jerusalem; and they were all scattered throughout the regions of Judea and Samaria, except the apostles.

Chapter 5 described the first flogging and here, in these verses, we have an account of the first Christian martyrdom. It was a scene that would be repeated in many different ways down the centuries.

We read of the complete uncontrolled frenzy of the court. We must never forget the anger that some non-believers have against the gospel and those who proclaim it. From the nature of the invective, we can only deduce that it was satanic. The term, "Gnashing of teeth", was used by Jesus to describe the eternal state of those who reject Him and the gospel. (Luke 13: 28) We must always remember that there is a heaven to be gained and a hell to be shunned.

We see the serenity of Stephen compared with the hateful violence of his executioners. We see here an example of the special grace and closeness of Jesus towards those of His people who suffer and those who are near the end of their lives. Stephen, like Peter, when on trial, had an infilling of the Holy Spirit.

During this unjust and barbaric execution, Stephen had a vision of heaven, with Jesus standing at the right hand of God. Stephen, who had earlier described himself as a believer in the "God of glory" could see the glory of God at this most critical moment. The term "Son of Man" is from the book of Daniel. It was a term Jesus used to describe Himself. It was a Messianic title and a divine title. Jesus' divinity was not similar to that which Romans gave to their emperors and heroes or that which we may confer on sporting greats, but was actual and eternal. He is from everlasting to everlasting. (Psalm 90: 2) He is the one by whom all things were made. (John 1: 3)

Stephen had an assurance that he was going to be with his Saviour. "Lord Jesus, receive my spirit." (v 59) There is no vision of purgatory, no uncertainty about what happens, but confidence in God's wonderful grace towards His people. Jesus is a loving Saviour, and although our faith may be weak, He has promised never to leave us: what a promise and what a hope! Although certain people may think that the doctrine of purgatory as taught by some is found in the Bible, there is no such evidence to support it. At the end of Stephen's life we have the delightful words, "He fell asleep." (v 60) Death for the Christian is not the end but a transit station in the progress of everlasting life.

We see a powerful picture of Stephen's loving nature. He prayed for his murderers: "Lord, do not hold this sin against them." Jesus was the only teacher who urged His followers to love their enemies, and pray for those who abuse us. (Mat 6:44) He prayed for those who crucified Him, "Father forgive them, for they do not know what they do." (Luke 23:34) Stephen followed in the footsteps of Jesus.

Finally, we are introduced to one who shared a common purpose with and held the coats of those who stoned Stephen. Stephen's prayer was answered in the life of this young, driven man. He was Saul of Tarsus. There is no doubt that Stephen and this violent event would remain in Paul's mind for the rest of his life. Years later, Paul would refer to himself as the chief of sinners. (1 Tim. 1:13-15)

Acts 8:2-8

2 And devout men carried Stephen to his burial, and made great lamentation over him. 3 As for Saul, he made havoc of the church, entering every house, and dragging off men and women, committing them to prison. 4 Therefore those who were scattered went everywhere preaching the word. 5 Then Philip went down to the city of Samaria and preached Christ to them. 6 And the multitudes with one accord heeded the things spoken by Philip, hearing and seeing the miracles which he did. 7 For unclean spirits, crying with a loud voice, came out of many who were possessed; and many who were paralyzed and lame were healed. 8 And there was great joy in that city.

Stephen was a gifted believer, highly intelligent, talented and full of love. No wonder the godly men, who buried him, mourned what they regarded as a catastrophic and irreplaceable loss.

This passage gives us a short insight into the first severe persecution that broke out after the death of Stephen. Although we are not specifically told, it appeared to be directed mainly at believers who were Greek-speaking Jews. The apostles managed to remain behind to care for those who were left. The ringleader of this persecution was Saul of Tarsus. He was thorough and ruthless, and Luke goes as far as to say that he began to destroy the church. Such was the radical nature of the violence that both women and men were dragged out of houses and put in prison. We should never forget that from the beginning of church history, women have been courageous, faithful witnesses and martyrs for Christ.

However, there was one effect that the persecutors had never thought of and that was geographical enlargement of the church. In the first chapter of Acts, Jesus said that they would be witnesses in Jerusalem, and all Judaea and Samaria, and to the ends of the Earth. This was being fulfilled in an unexpected way. The Holy

Spirit is full of surprises. Paradoxically, the spread of the church was achieved through vicious persecution.

Samaritans were a people of mixed ancestry, and Jews had no dealings with the Samaritans. (John 4: 9) During His ministry, Jesus opened His hand out to a number of Samaritans. As far as Jesus was concerned, they would be welcome into His kingdom.

We have already met Philip, who, like Stephen, was one of the diaconate appointments. They began their Christian service with what some might regard as mundane, routine service. They were willing servants. Many well-known Christians have been willing in their ministry to do those administrative tasks that many would regard as beneath them. Filling in papers, putting out chairs, cleaning toilets are all part of the Lord's work.

Well done, good and faithful servant; you were faithful over a few things, I will make you ruler over many things. Enter into the joy of your lord. (Mat 25: 21)

As a Greek-speaking Jew with knowledge of other cultures, Philip was just the man for the job of preaching to the inhabitants of Samaria. He is the only man in the Bible given the title "Evangelist." We note three points about his ministry in that place.

Firstly, he proclaimed or preached Christ to them. They would, no doubt, have heard stories of Jesus, and His travels, even through Samaria. A woman had made a statement, many months before, "Could this be the Christ?" (John 4:29) Philip emphasized that Jesus was the Messiah, and preached to them about the cross, the resurrection of Jesus and the need for repentance. As well as being an evangelist, he displayed the apostolic gift of signs, wonders and healings. This caused the people to pay close attention to what he said.

Secondly, let us never neglect the ministry of preaching. We should all pay close attention to the contents of sermons. Preachers should always have before them the great responsibility they bear. They need to prepare themselves by living exemplary lives, and work diligently on the content and delivery of their words. Moreover, they and we must pray that God will fill them with the Holy Spirit, every time they speak. We may not all be evangelists with a capital E, but we are all able to speak for Christ, and give a reason for the hope that we have. We can do no greater favour to anyone than to tell him or her about Jesus, even if they do not think it a favour.

These persecuted believers, many of whom were thrown out of their homes, became refugees. However, they never ceased to talk about their new-found faith.

Finally, there was great joy in that city. (v 8) The Gospels do not state anywhere that Jesus laughed. He may well have laughed but the writers, through the Holy Spirit, do not include it. I think this is because He wanted to identify Himself with those who were in trouble. He "came to seek and to save that which was lost." (Luke 19:10)

Nevertheless, we are told that He was full of joy on return of the seventy from their mission:

In that hour Jesus rejoiced in the Spirit and said, "I thank You, Father, Lord of heaven and earth, that You have hidden these things from the wise and prudent and revealed them to babes." (Luke 10: 21)

Furthermore, the disciples were glad or overjoyed when they saw the risen Lord Jesus. (John 20:20) The joy of the Lord is a deep contentment leading to expressions of praise and often with great exultation, as in this passage. So often, little joy may be due to little commitment on the part of the believer.

Acts 8:9-13

9 But there was a certain man called Simon, who previously practiced sorcery in the city and astonished the people of Samaria, claiming that he was someone great, 10 to whom they all gave heed, from the least to the greatest, saying, "This man is the great power of God." 11 And they heeded him because he had astonished them with his sorceries for a long time. 12 But when they believed Philip as he preached the things concerning the kingdom of God and the name of Jesus Christ, both men and women were baptized. 13 Then Simon himself also believed; and when he was baptized he continued with Philip, and was amazed, seeing the miracles and signs which were done.

This passage needs to be read carefully by all Christians and studied by all who are in the role of leadership. There is a clear statement concerning the baptism of many believers, and an introduction to a man known as Simon the sorcerer.

There are a number of things we should mark in this passage. We should mark that the people of Samaria believed as Philip preached the good news of the kingdom of God and the name of Jesus Christ. (v 12) They did not believe in an assortment of religious thoughts but key truths about Jesus and salvation. We must ask ourselves if we are repentant and in godly sorrow for our sins. Do we renounce evil and the devil? Do we believe that Jesus had died in our place as a punishment and sacrifice for sin? Do we trust in Christ and His righteousness for our salvation? Jesus warned, "Narrow is the gate and difficult is the way which leads to life, and there are few who find it." (Matt 7: 14)

We should mark, secondly, the natural willingness of many to be deceived by false teachers. Even in our secular age, many spend part or much of their lives reading horoscopes and are attentive to "New Age " spiritualities. Bookshops are full of it, and newspapers have their astrology sections. At best they are a deception and at worst a demonic entrance into people's thinking. Even on a natural day-to-day level, we are all susceptible to many kinds of "scams", usually financial. Some so-called televangelists have deceived people for monetary gain. The success of Simon, with all his magic and incantations, led him to accept the title "the Great Power of God". (v 10) He put himself in the place of God. In contrast, Paul referred to the gospel as, "The power of God to salvation for everyone who believes." (Rom 1: 16) Later Christian writers referred to Simon as the arch heretic of the church and the "Father" of Gnostic teaching.

We should mark, thirdly, that Simon the sorcerer appeared to be a believer, and would have been regarded as a celebrity convert. He seemed to be enthusiastic. He followed Philip everywhere. He was baptized when he said that he believed. It is distressing but true that there are those who are baptized and yet are not true believers. Baptism does not of itself confer grace. True belief in Christ is necessary. Many faithful ministers of the gospel have baptized people who later abandoned their faith. It is a cause of sadness, but when done in good faith should not be a cause for blame. Philip baptized Simon the sorcerer, trusting that he was genuine.

We should mark finally that once again Luke conferred a respected status on women. He noted that they were part of the persecution in and from Jerusalem. In Samaria, both men and women are baptized. It reinforces the statement that Christ died for all, and that, "There is neither Jew nor Greek, there is neither slave nor free, there is neither male nor female; for you are all one in Christ Jesus." (Gal 3: 28)

Acts 8:14-25

14 Now when the apostles who were at Jerusalem heard that Samaria had received the word of God, they sent Peter and John to them, **15** who, when they had come down, prayed for them that they might receive the Holy Spirit. **16** For as yet He had fallen upon none of them. They had only been baptized in the name of the Lord Jesus. **17** Then they laid hands on them, and they received the Holy Spirit. **18** And when Simon saw that through the laying on of the apostles' hands the Holy Spirit was given, he offered them money, **19** saying, "Give me this power also, that anyone on whom I lay hands may receive the Holy Spirit." **20** But Peter said to him, "Your money perish with you, because you thought that the gift of God could be purchased with money! **21** You have neither part nor portion in this matter, for your heart is not right in the sight of God. **22** Repent therefore of this your wickedness, and pray God if perhaps the thought of your heart may be forgiven you. **23** For I see that you are poisoned by bitterness and bound by iniquity." **24** Then Simon answered and said, "Pray to the Lord for me, that none of the things which you have spoken may come upon me." **25** So when they had testified and preached the word of the Lord, they returned to Jerusalem, preaching the gospel in many villages of the Samaritans.

In this passage, there are two contrasting themes. The first one is the gift of the Holy Spirit to the believers in Samaria. This was through the laying-on of hands by the Apostles, Peter and John. The second was the threat posed by Simon the sorcerer to a fledgling Samaritan church.

Peter and John were no doubt intrigued by what was going on in Samaria, so they left the crisis in Jerusalem to find out for themselves the events in that part of the country. They saw that the Samaritans had truly believed, and the apostles brought more joy to the city when they laid hands on them to receive the Holy Spirit. The Samaritans who up till then had been the despised half-breeds were now in full equal fellowship with the believers in Jerusalem.

The universal tendency to despise and be suspicious of those who are of different race, nation or social group is far too prevalent in the church. We need to take our example from those early God-led Apostles.

We are not told the nature of the Holy Spirit manifestation on these believers but it certainly impressed Simon the sorcerer, and at this point he demonstrated his true heart.

It is not easy to detect false believers and it is necessary not to rush to early judgement. In so doing, we may throw off a number of genuine if eccentric and unusual converts. The characteristics shown by Simon are as follows.

Firstly, he became a believer not because he was convicted, but because he wanted to use and exploit God for his own ends. He did not wish to be a true servant of Christ. He desired to impress others by his magic. He wanted to use his apparent faith to manipulate the vulnerable and gain wealth.

Secondly, he thought God's gift could be purchased with money. There are some in this world who believe it possible to buy anything with money. "Everyone has his price." God's salvation is without price and cannot be purchased. It is a free gift. The Christian should be wary of those who are in ministry to amass vast fortunes on account of it. Fortunately, such people are rare.

Thirdly, after Peter's reprimand, Simon asked that God's judgement should not come on him. He showed no repentance or any kind of change. He was all right, it was up to Peter to use his "hotline" to God and fix things for him. (v 24)

Preachers need to make regular references to the need for true repentance. Paul makes the distinction between Godly sorrow and worldly sorrow:

For godly sorrow produces repentance leading to salvation, not to be regretted; but the sorrow of the world produces death. (2 Cor 7: 10)

True repentance brings a turn round in attitude, and is thankful to God because everything is totally forgiven. Worldly sorrow says, "Never again," and within a short space of time resumes the old routine and excesses.

Finally, Simon experienced a great feeling of jealously. Such emotions can be felt by anyone at anytime. A believer can counter this by knowing that he or she is special and precious to God and each one has their own function in the church and work of God. The false believer, deep down, has no such assurance.

Acts 8:26-40

26 Now an angel of the Lord spoke to Philip, saying, "Arise and go toward the south along the road which goes down from Jerusalem to Gaza." This is desert. **27** So he arose and went. And behold, a man of Ethiopia, a eunuch of great authority under Candace the queen of the Ethiopians, who had charge of all her treasury, and had come to Jerusalem to worship, **28** was returning. And sitting in his chariot, he was reading Isaiah the prophet. **29** Then the Spirit said to Philip, "Go near and overtake this chariot." **30** So Philip ran to him, and heard him reading the prophet Isaiah, and said, "Do you understand what you are reading?" **31** And he said, "How can I, unless someone guides me?" And he asked Philip to come up and sit with him. **32** The place in the Scripture which he read was this: "He was led as a sheep to the slaughter; And as a lamb before its shearer is silent, So He opened not His mouth. **33** In His humiliation His justice was taken away, And who will declare His generation? For His life is taken from the earth." **34** So the eunuch answered Philip and said, "I ask you, of whom does the prophet say this, of himself or of some other man?" **35** Then Philip opened his mouth, and beginning at this Scripture, preached Jesus to him. **36** Now as they went down the road, they came to some water. And the eunuch said, "See, here is water. What hinders me from being baptized?" **37** Then Philip said, "If you believe with all your heart, you may." And he answered and said, "I believe that Jesus Christ is the Son of God." **38** So he commanded the chariot to stand still. And both Philip and the eunuch went down into the water, and he baptized him. **39** Now when they came up out of the water, the Spirit of the Lord caught Philip away, so that the eunuch saw him no more; and he went on his way rejoicing. **40** But Philip was found at Azotus. And passing through, he preached in all the cities till he came to Caesarea.

The conversion of the Ethiopian finance minister provides the Christian with a treasury of information.

Firstly, we see the unusual obedience of Philip. There he was in the middle of a revival with a stack of work to do and many needs around him. Yet he was taken away to a remote place to talk to a VIP whom he had never met before; how inconvenient, yet how typical of the Holy Spirit. We may think that a certain direction is the right way to go; yet God takes us on another, and paradoxically with even greater blessing. Furthermore, God uses busy people! He does not tend to use people who loaf around and wait for things to happen.

Secondly, because he was a member of Queen Candace's court and in spite of his high rank, the Ethiopian was emasculated. Therefore was excluded from the temple rituals and worship. He was not even allowed to convert to Judaism, or become what was known as a true proselyte. However, like many in those days, he was attracted to Judaism from the beliefs in a panoply of capricious gods. There was something ethical, ordered and calm about Judaism and its belief in one moral creator God. Throughout history, there have been individuals who have been attracted in some way to Christ. And they must not be left in that situation. They must be encouraged to truly find Him and come to Him and trust in Him as both Saviour and Lord.

Thirdly, the Ethiopian did a wise thing in obtaining a copy of the Scripture and in particular the prophecy of Isaiah. We do not know if he bought one or was given one but he made sure he had one. Many have spoken of how the reading of the Bible has been an important milestone in their journey to faith in Christ. We can give no more valuable gift to anyone than a copy of the Scriptures. Do we read it? Do we take it to heart? Do we treasure God's Word?

Fourthly, we see one of God's sovereign incidents in the words he 'just happened' to be reading. Isaiah 53 is a key passage in our understanding of the whole purpose and ministry of Jesus. Parts of it are quoted or referred to over twenty-five times in the New Testament; such is its importance.

When a "not yet Christian" reads parts of the Bible, the text can be totally baffling. That is why help is needed; that's why we need a preacher. The Ethiopian would not have known that the passage in Isaiah was about the Lord Jesus. That Jesus was the suffering servant who took the wrath of God upon Himself. He was the one who was punished in our place. Through Jesus' sacrifice, we may be forgiven. "By his stripes we are healed." (Isa. 53: 5) Philip did not miss the opportunity to explain the gospel to this man. In spite of its apparent foolishness, the Lord's sacrificial death on the cross, leading to our forgiveness is vital. Many preachers miss this point. Sadly for them and their hearers, many do not even believe it.

Just as God had led Philip to that place, God had prepared the heart of the eunuch. He was baptized. Now he was not excluded by his race and surgical condition from the gathering of the people of God. He was included in the company of God's people, a company that would one day stretch around the world. Just as the people of Samaria rejoiced, this Gentile with his new found-faith went on his way rejoicing.

Acts 9:1-7

1 Then Saul, still breathing threats and murder against the disciples of the Lord, went to the high priest **2** and asked letters from him to the synagogues of Damascus, so that if he found any who were of the Way, whether men or women, he might bring them bound to Jerusalem. **3** As he journeyed he came near Damascus, and suddenly a light shone around him from heaven. **4** Then he fell to the ground, and heard a voice saying to him, "Saul, Saul, why are you persecuting Me?" **5** And he said, "Who are You, Lord?" Then the Lord said, "I am Jesus, whom you are persecuting. It is hard for you to kick against the goads." **6** So he, trembling and astonished, said, "Lord, what do You want me to do?" Then the Lord said to him, "Arise and go into the city, and you will be told what you must do." **7** And the men who journeyed with him stood speechless, hearing a voice but seeing no one.

The conversion of Saul of Tarsus is one of the most significant events in human history. When Saul set off from Jerusalem with letters from the high priest to persecute believers in Damascus, he was a highly intelligent, highly educated, quick-tempered, cruel, zealous religionist. When he arrived in Damascus, he was an overpowered, blind and subdued shadow of a man.

One thing we can note is that Paul's experience of conversion on the road not far from Damascus was the most dramatic of all conversions. We may not experience a flash of light, later described as brighter than the noonday sun. (Acts 26: 13) We may not fall to the ground, or be blinded, or hear the voice of Jesus. Our conversion to Christ may be sudden or the culmination of a period of time, but the result of all true conversions is that we are humbled and call Jesus 'Lord'. Not only do we say, 'Lord' - we mean it.

Secondly, it is moving to note that if anyone harms or persecutes a Christian, they are persecuting none other than the Lord

Jesus Himself. "Saul, Saul, why are you persecuting Me?" (v 4) Sometimes we may not think so, but we are precious in the eyes of God, even though we may have to endure hardships and all kinds of trouble, just as our Lord did.

Thirdly, many have tried to explain away the conversion of Paul. One explanation is that a bolt of lightning struck him. While such an event might have blinded him, he would also have suffered more serious injuries also. Furthermore, his companions would have witnessed the lightning.

Perhaps the most prevalent explanation is that he suffered an epileptic fit, which accounts for his later reference to a "thorn in the flesh." We have no evidence of epilepsy in Saul's life, although some authorities indicate that there are a number of people with temporal lobe epilepsy who have marked religious feelings. Saul, or rather Paul would later describe his conversion on more than one occasion, and we do know that those who have fits usually have no memory of them at all. Moreover, an epileptic fit does not normally turn a life around. I like the remarks of one commentator who said that if this was due to epilepsy, then, "blessed epilepsy!"

Finally, this experience on the Damascus road was much more than a vision. Later, Paul said that he had actually seen the risen, ascended and glorified Christ, and that this validated his apostleship.

For I delivered to you first of all that which I also received: that Christ died for our sins according to the Scriptures, and that He was buried, and that He rose again the third day according to the Scriptures, and that He was seen by Cephas, then by the twelve. After that He was seen by over five hundred brethren at once, of whom the greater part remain to the present, but some have fallen asleep. After that He was seen by James, then by all the apostles. Then last of all He was seen by me also, as by one born out of due time. For I am the least of the apostles, who am not worthy to be called an apostle, because I persecuted the church of God. But by the grace of God I am what I am, and His grace toward me was not in vain; but I labored more abundantly than they all, yet not I, but the grace of God which was with me. Therefore, whether it was I or they, so we preach and so you believed. (1 Cor. 15: 3-11)

This conversion on the Damascus road had implications that are with us to this day. Instead of remaining what some would have described as a Jewish sect, faith in Christ became a worldwide movement. In addition, Paul wrote a large part of the New Testament, which continues to be a world bestseller.

Acts 9:8-19

8 Then Saul arose from the ground, and when his eyes were opened he saw no one. But they led him by the hand and brought him into Damascus. **9** And he was three days without sight, and neither ate nor drank. **10** Now there was a certain disciple at Damascus named Ananias; and to him the Lord said in a vision, "Ananias." And he said, "Here I am, Lord." **11** So the Lord said to him, "Arise and go to the street called Straight, and inquire at the house of Judas for one called Saul of Tarsus, for behold, he is praying. **12** And in a vision he has seen a man named Ananias coming in and putting his hand on him, so that he might receive his sight." **13** Then Ananias answered, "Lord, I have heard from many about this man, how much harm he has done to Your saints in Jerusalem. **14** And here he has authority from the chief priests to bind all who call on Your name." **15** But the Lord said to him, "Go, for he is a chosen vessel of Mine to bear My name before Gentiles, kings, and the children of Israel. **16** For I will show him how many things he must suffer for My name's sake." **17** And Ananias went his way and entered the house; and laying his hands on him he said, "Brother Saul, the Lord Jesus, who appeared to you on the road as you came, has sent me that you may receive your sight and be filled with the Holy Spirit." **18** Immediately there fell from his eyes something like scales, and he received his sight at once; and he arose and was baptized. **19** So when he had received food, he was strengthened. Then Saul spent some days with the disciples at Damascus.

This passage refers to two principal players. Ananias has a walk-on part in the book of Acts, the other, Saul of Tarsus later became the dominant human character.

Here, Paul was a broken man, who played a somewhat passive role. Perhaps he felt that in view of his crimes, he should have been struck dead on the road. However, since he had survived, and no doubt aware of the content of some of Stephen's arguments, he knew also that he was being forgiven.

No longer did he breathe lethal threats; he was peaceful. He was praying, was baptised, had hands laid on him, and scales fell from his eyes. It reinforces the fact that when we become Christians, we may think we are doing something, but it is principally what is being done for us and to us. The Holy Spirit calls, convicts, leads, and then comes into our lives to change us; something which Paul would repeatedly teach in his writings. (Eph. 2:5)

Ananias demonstrated a close fellowship with God. God was able to use him in a special way to welcome Saul into the community of believers. Since Ananias was a particularly devout believer, he was no doubt number one on the Damascus persecution hit list. Instead of being taken away in chains, he was the one who befriended, baptized and laid hands on this extraordinary convert.

Ananias had words from God, which demonstrated the depth of Paul's ministry and the people to whom he would testify. Moreover, Ananias, although a devout Jewish believer, understood and welcomed the fact that the Gentiles would be part of this new development in Christianity (v 15)

This passage underlines the courage and faith of Ananias. He was prepared to take a big risk in order to fulfil this task for God. He had made up his mind to be obedient to God. There are very few risk takers for God. People are prepared to risk enormous things for money, position and fame, but barely a pound coin for God. We should be people of prayer to find out God's will for our lives, and people of courage to do God's will.

Finally, we see here the great kindness shown by Ananias. He was not cold and grudging in his mission to visit and welcome this former scourge of the church. He was warm, generous and encouraging towards Saul. He put himself out for this new convert. It is an attitude we should all copy.

Acts 9:20-30

20 Immediately he preached the Christ in the synagogues, that He is the Son of God. **21** Then all who heard were amazed, and said, "Is this not he who destroyed those who called on this name in Jerusalem, and has come here for that purpose, so that he might bring them bound to the chief priests?" **22** But Saul increased all the more in strength, and confounded the Jews who dwelt in Damascus, proving that this Jesus is the Christ. **23** Now after many days were past, the Jews plotted to kill him. **24** But their plot became known to Saul. And they watched the gates day and night, to kill him. **25** Then the disciples took him by night and let him down through the wall in a large basket. **26** And when Saul had come to Jerusalem, he tried to join the disciples; but they were all afraid of him, and did not believe that he was a disciple. **27** But Barnabas took him and brought him to the apostles. And he declared to them how he had seen the Lord on the road, and that He had spoken to him, and how he had preached boldly at Damascus in the name of Jesus. **28** So he was with them at Jerusalem, coming in and going out. **29** And he spoke boldly in the name of the Lord Jesus and disputed against the Hellenists, but they attempted to kill him. **30** When the brethren found out, they brought him down to Caesarea and sent him out to Tarsus.

Saul's role reversal from persecutor to proclaimer perplexed the Jews in Damascus and later those in Jerusalem. No wonder, since the former archenemy and troubler of Christians had changed direction so completely. Conversion to Christ is often puzzling to family and friends. Is it real? Will it last? Is it welcomed? Sometimes friends leave, or follow our example, or stubbornly remain indifferent. Whatever the consequences, and so far as it is in our control, we should stay as loyal to our families as we are able.

Saul, now Spirit filled, soon went on the move and he began to declare that Jesus was not only "the Christ" or the Messiah, but also the "Son of God". This Divine title was the first time in Acts that it was stated directly. It is important that we understand what this meant.

The Old Testament referred to Israel as God's son. Later, the king is denoted as a son. The Romans referred to the emperor as God's son. The New Testament took the meaning much further. Paul later wrote that Jesus was declared to be Son of God by His resurrection. (Rom 1: 3-4) He also described Jesus as follows:

He is the image of the invisible God, the firstborn over all creation. For by Him all things were created that are in heaven and that are on earth, visible and invisible, whether thrones or dominions or principalities or powers. All things were created through Him and for Him. And He is before all things, and in Him all things consist. (Col 1: 15-17)

It is possible to think too little of Christ, but no-one has esteemed Christ too highly. Our understanding of Christ's worth has profound and eternal consequences. Is He our Saviour? Is He our Lord? Do we love Him?

The consequences of Paul's love and devotion stirred up an opposition, which was a starter for the rest of his life. When he left Damascus, it was in the humiliation of being lowered through an opening in the wall in a basket.

In Jerusalem there was similar bewilderment and fear of this new convert. Here, Barnabas returned to the scene. He saw the reality of the change in Saul's life, his genius, and also his potential. With great courage and kindness, he introduced Saul to the Apostles, which confirmed in Saul's mind the accuracy of his teaching. Saul's clear and outspoken debates with the Grecian Jews soon landed him in trouble. As in Damascus, they wanted to kill him. Barnabas quickly bundled him off via Caesarea to Tarsus, a journey of around five hundred miles. We do not know the extent of Saul's hardships in Jerusalem and Tarsus, but he was being prepared for all the privations of his future ministry.

When we become a Christian, we are promised forgiveness, eternal salvation and a new life. We are not promised a spouse, a house, a job, wealth or health, although we may be given such things. It is important for preachers to make this clear. It is important to become a believer for the right reasons. If we do not, then a fall away becomes almost inevitable. Jesus said, "Foxes have holes and birds of the air have nests, but the Son of Man has nowhere to lay his head." (Luke 9: 58) Furthermore, we must be on guard that our status and possessions do not make us flabby and half-heated Christians. Jesus wrote a warning to the church in Laodicea:

Because you say, 'I am rich, have become wealthy, and have need of nothing' and do not know that you are wretched, miserable, poor, blind, and naked. I counsel you to buy from Me gold refined in the fire, that you may be rich; and white garments, that you may be clothed, that the shame of your nakedness may not be revealed; and anoint your eyes with eye salve, that you may see. (Rev 3:17-18)

It is so easy to rely on possessions and make our treasure there, rather than in the kingdom of God.

Acts 9:31-43

31 Then the churches throughout all Judea, Galilee, and Samaria had peace and were edified. And walking in the fear of the Lord and in the comfort of the Holy Spirit, they were multiplied. **32** Now it came to pass, as Peter went through all parts of the country, that he also came down to the saints who dwelt in Lydda. **33** There he found a certain man named Aeneas, who had been bedridden eight years and was paralyzed. **34** And Peter said to him, "Aeneas, Jesus the Christ heals you. Arise and make your bed." Then he arose immediately. **35** So all who dwelt at Lydda and Sharon saw him and turned to the Lord. **36** At Joppa there was a certain disciple named Tabitha, which is translated Dorcas. This woman was full of good works and charitable deeds which she did. **37** But it happened in those days that she became sick and died. When they had washed her, they laid her in an upper room. **38** And since Lydda was near Joppa, and the disciples had heard that Peter was there, they sent two men to him, imploring him not to delay in coming to them. **39** Then Peter arose and went with them. When he had come, they brought him to the upper room. And all the widows stood by him weeping, showing the tunics and garments which Dorcas had made while she was with them. **40** But Peter put them all out, and knelt down and prayed. And turning to the body he said, "Tabitha, arise." And she opened her eyes, and when she saw Peter she sat up. **41** Then he gave her his hand and lifted her up; and when he had called the saints and widows, he presented her alive. **42** And it became known throughout all Joppa, and many believed on the Lord. **43** So it was that he stayed many days in Joppa with Simon, a tanner.

The geographical expansion as a result of the havoc instigated by Saul led to numerical expansion achieved as a consequence of the witness of those new settlers. The description of Peter's ministry moved from preaching to large crowds and the Sanhedrin to local and personal pastoral care. Comparatively few are good at both forms of ministry, but both are of great importance. Many a fine speaker has neglected personal ministry to the cost of many in their churches.

The healing of Aeneas is remarkable, and is mentioned by Luke because of its extraordinary nature, and unlike the antics of local faith healers. We need to note that the miracles carried out in both the Gospels and Acts are not public spectaculars as Jesus was tempted to do, but acts of compassion for needy and broken human beings.

This miracle was typical of others and showed certain properties. Firstly, these were genuine physical conditions, which had been resistant to any form of treatment. This man Aeneas had been paralysed and bedridden for eight years. Secondly, no other effective treatment was being carried out at the time. Thirdly, the cure was instantaneous. He required no rehabilitation. Lastly, as far as we know, the cure was permanent. No wonder the local people were amazed and many believed in Jesus. As is typical in Peter's ministry, he deflected any attention and praise from himself to the Lord.

The next episode of pastoral care concerned a dead woman, and Peter responded immediately to a request to come at once. It is a great gift to know when to drop everything in response to a specific need.

In these verses, we are reminded of the reign of death that is on this earth. We keep on thinking that death happens to others, until we ourselves are given news of a fatal illness. Death is the last enemy. It happens to rich and poor alike. It does not spare the young, beautiful and gifted, or the tireless and generous Christian woman. There are few griefs worse than the loss of a child, partner or dear friend. So often, we know and feel there is nothing we can do about it.

Peter was in a situation that was similar to one many months before, when Jesus raised the daughter of Jairus. (Luke 8: 49-56) Peter cleared the room of people, knelt by the bed and prayed. He spoke to the corpse, and then helped Dorcas up by the hand.

There are five specific cases described in the New Testament where people have been raised from the dead. All these individuals ultimately died. Nevertheless, they are a glimpse or preview of the day our Lord returns, and the dead in Christ will be raised. There will be no more tears, no more death, and no more funerals.

Before leaving this passage, it is worth remarking on the service, which Dorcas gave to the community. She used her gifts to help others, and particularly those in need. Christians down the centuries have helped others in similar ways. Whilst these acts of service do not save us, they are a consequence of faith in Christ, and a reflection of His love. It is the sort of thing that lifts people's lives and helps many find faith.

Finally, we are told that Peter stayed in the House of Simon the tanner. Such an occupation required work with animal carcases and was considered unclean, and therefore both the location and the workers were unclean. Peter did not stay in great houses but in this humble home. Some have remarked about the lack of contemporary literature about the beginnings of the church from non-Christian sources. It really is not surprising since most believers at that time were such ordinary people.

Jesus in his parable of the "Great Banquet" talked about a certain man who sent out numerous invitations to supposedly respectable people who all in turn refused. Jesus then said:

So that servant came and reported these things to his master. Then the master of the house, being angry, said to his servant, 'Go out quickly into the streets and lanes of the city, and bring in here the poor and the maimed and the lame and the blind (Luke 14: 21)

The early church was composed of such people as our Lord described.

Acts 10:1-7

1 There was a certain man in Caesarea called Cornelius, a centurion of what was called the Italian Regiment, 2 a devout man and one who feared God with all his household, who gave alms generously to the people, and prayed to God always. 3 About the ninth hour of the day he saw clearly in a vision an angel of God coming in and saying to him, "Cornelius!" 4 And when he observed him, he was afraid, and said, "What is it, lord?" So he said to him, "Your prayers and your alms have come up for a memorial before God. 5 Now send men to Joppa, and send for Simon whose surname is Peter. 6 He is lodging with Simon, a tanner, whose house is by the sea. He will tell you what you must do." 7 And when the angel who spoke to him had departed, Cornelius called two of his household servants and a devout soldier from among those who waited on him continually.

This chapter deals with a momentous move in the history of the church. Although Peter had already discarded some Jewish prejudices when he ministered to the Samaritans and stayed at the house of a tanner, there was one prejudice that required a massive change in his mind-set. The Jewish attitude to non-Jews was a deeply entrenched attitude that was shared throughout the country. To him and others, the world was securely divided into two groups of people, Jews and Gentiles. The Jews were part of God's community, and Gentiles were not. They would not go into a Gentile house or eat with them; such was the antipathy. Similarly, the vast majority of Gentiles despised the Jews, their beliefs and customs.

There was a slight crack in this wall of separation in that some Gentiles became proselytes, but these people had to take on all the laws, rituals and customs of the Jews. Generally speaking, the gulf of separation was impregnable. Another crack in the wall is the notable attraction that some Gentiles had towards Judaism, in spite of all the prejudice against them. Such an attraction even came from those hated occupiers, the ranks of the Roman army. Roman centurions were amongst the hard men of the Roman military. They were the enforcers. Yet they receive a "good press" in the New Testament, and our Lord was very kind to Roman soldiers. Amongst His last words, as Romans were nailing Him to a cross, were, "Father forgive them, for they do not know what they do." (Luke 23: 34)

Cornelius was truly remarkable. He and his family were devout. He gave to the poor, and he prayed regularly. Some soldiers under his command were also devout. He feared God. God rewarded his diligence and a sovereign movement of the Holy Spirit was working in his life.

We should note the kindness of the centurion. He would not have learnt this from the military. Roman tribunes, consuls and prefects and emperors would not have encouraged such an attitude. We can only conclude that it was the Holy Spirit working on his life. Like the centurion, we should show kindness to all with whom we come into contact. This is the one way to recommend our faith. It is something every-one can understand. Kindness was a feature of our Lord's character, and we should ask ourselves regularly, "What is the kind thing to do in this situation?"

Those who become Christians are usually those who begin to exercise belief and develop a sense of the holiness of God, and an awareness of the righteous judgement of God. God is the rewarder of those who seek Him with all their hearts.(Hebrews 11:6) Most in the West have no reverence for God. He is an optional extra to a self-indulgent world-view. In spite of all this, there are those who know their need of God and respond to His call.

Acts 10:8-23

8 So when he had explained all these things to them, he sent them to Joppa. 9 The next day, as they went on their journey and drew near the city, Peter went up on the housetop to pray, about the sixth hour. 10 Then he became very hungry and wanted to eat; but while they made ready, he fell into a trance 11 and saw heaven opened and an object like a great sheet bound at the four corners, descending to him and let down to the earth. 12 In it were all kinds of four-footed animals of the earth, wild beasts, creeping things, and birds of the air. 13 And a voice came to him, "Rise, Peter; kill and eat." 14 But Peter said, "Not so, Lord! For I have never eaten anything common or unclean." 15 And a voice spoke to him again the second time, "What God has cleansed you must not call common." 16 This was done three times. And the object was taken up into heaven again. 17 Now while Peter wondered within himself what this vision which he had seen meant, behold, the men who had been sent from Cornelius had made inquiry for Simon's house, and stood before the gate. 18 And they called and asked whether Simon, whose surname was Peter, was lodging there. 19 While Peter thought about the vision, the Spirit said to him, "Behold, three men are seeking you. 20 Arise therefore, go down and go with them, doubting nothing; for I have sent them." 21 Then Peter went down to the men who had been sent to him from Cornelius, and said, "Yes, I am he whom you seek. For what reason have you come?" 22 And they said, "Cornelius the centurion, a just man, one who fears God and has a good reputation among all the nation of the Jews, was divinely instructed by a holy angel to summon you to his house, and to hear words from you." 23 Then he invited them in and lodged them. On the next day Peter went away with them, and some brethren from Joppa accompanied him.

Luke takes much time and effort in describing the details of these events. It was such a significant step for everyone, not least Peter himself. There are comparatively few verses that describe the healing of Aeneas and the raising to life of Dorcas, and yet a whole section is set aside to describe the change of a deep-seated prejudice.

Just as Cornelius was praying, so was Peter. The vision on the roof was significant for a number of reasons. The invitation to get up and eat both clean and unclean animals was totally contrary to Peter's long established mind-set. The stipulations in the law concerning animals that could and could not be eaten had good reasons medically, but more than that, it separated the people of Israel from the surrounding nations. They were chosen to be a people that took no part in pagan and idolatrous practices. (Lev 17) However, the vision signified the coming together of Jews and Gentiles. Peter had to be told three times, which was reminiscent of the occasion when Peter denied his Lord three times, (John 18: 15-27) and also when Jesus asked Peter three times, "Do you love me?"(John 21: 15-17) The arrival of Cornelius' men at the door confirmed in Peter's mind that his attitude had to change.

It is worth remarking that the angel did not suggest to Cornelius that a delegation should go round to Philip the evangelist's house that was nearby, but travel to Joppa. It was crucially important that there had to be a transformation in the mind of Peter, the leading pastor and Apostle. Paul later wrote:

There is neither Jew nor Greek, there is neither slave nor free, there is neither male nor female; for you are all one in Christ Jesus. And if you are Christ's, then you are Abraham's seed, and heirs according to the promise. (Gal 3: 28-29)

Most of us do not experience visions, and usually we call them hallucinations, since they may be part of a mental illness. Although we should exercise caution when such claims are made, we should respect them. It may be the only way that God can get through. In parts of the Middle East and North Africa, a number of people have become Christian through experiencing visions of Christ.

Finally, we all have prejudices. It was not until the sixteenth century that it was thought permissible for all to read the Bible in their own language. It was not until the nineteenth century that that the slave trade was abolished. It was not thought necessary to evangelize the whole world until the late eighteenth and early nineteenth centuries. We all have a tendency to harbour negative feelings towards people from different nations, races, backgrounds and denominations. It takes many lessons to even recognize these prejudices, and more to act on them. We should all ask God to show us where we fall short and give us the intention, courage and strength to change. In Peter's case, the first move was the invitation Peter gave to the visiting Gentiles to enter the house where he was staying.

Acts 10:24-48

24 And the following day they entered Caesarea. Now Cornelius was waiting for them, and had called together his relatives and close friends. **25** As Peter was coming in, Cornelius met him and fell down at his feet and worshiped him. **26** But Peter lifted him up, saying, "Stand up; I myself am also a man." **27** And as he talked with him, he went in and found many who had come together. **28** Then he said to them, "You know how unlawful it is for a Jewish man to keep company with or go to one of another nation. But God has shown me that I should not call any man common or unclean. **29** Therefore I came without objection as soon as I was sent for. I ask, then, for what reason have you sent for me?" **30** So Cornelius said, "Four days ago I was fasting until this hour; and at the ninth hour I prayed in my house, and behold, a man stood before me in bright clothing, **31** and said, 'Cornelius, your prayer has been heard, and your alms are remembered in the sight of God. **32** Send therefore to Joppa and call Simon here, whose surname is Peter. He is lodging in the house of Simon, a tanner, by the sea. When he comes, he will speak to you.' **33** So I sent to you immediately, and you have done well to come. Now therefore, we are all present before God, to hear all the things commanded you by God." **34** Then Peter opened his mouth and said: "In truth I perceive that God shows no partiality. **35** But in every nation whoever fears Him and works righteousness is accepted by Him. **36** The word which God sent to the children of Israel, preaching peace through Jesus Christ--He is Lord of all-- **37** that word you know, which was proclaimed throughout all Judea, and began from Galilee after the baptism which John preached: **38** how God anointed Jesus of Nazareth with the Holy Spirit and with power, who went about doing good and healing all who were oppressed by the devil, for God was with Him. **39** And we are witnesses of all things which He did both in the land of the Jews and in Jerusalem, whom they killed by hanging on a tree. **40** Him God raised up on the third day, and showed Him openly, **41** not to all the people, but to witnesses chosen before by God, even to us who ate and drank with Him after He arose from the dead. **42** And He commanded us to preach to the people, and to testify that it is He who was ordained by God to be Judge of the living and the dead. **43** To Him all the prophets witness that, through His name, whoever believes in Him will receive remission of sins." **44** While Peter was still speaking these words, the Holy Spirit fell upon all those who heard the word. **45** And those of the circumcision who believed were astonished, as many as came with Peter, because the gift of the Holy Spirit had been poured out on the Gentiles also. **46** For they heard them speak with tongues and magnify God. Then Peter answered, **47** "Can anyone forbid water, that these should not be baptized who have received the Holy Spirit just as we have?" **48** And he commanded them to be baptized in the name of the Lord. Then they asked him to stay a few days.

Peter must have been surprised when he arrived to find a large group of people waiting for him. We may not have a great apostle coming to preach on Sunday but do we wait in expectation that God will have something special to say to us each Sunday? It may be in the hymns, prayers or sermon, but we should all ask the question: "What has God taught me today?"

When Peter entered the house, Cornelius fell at his feet. It is easy to give worship and praise to men and it is also easy for gifted men to accept it. Peter would have none of it. "Stand up; I myself am also a man." (v 26) Popes, prelates and pop stars - please note!The message Peter spoke was of great importance. We should note what he did not say as well as what he did say.

Peter commended his hearers for their fear of God and their endeavours to do good, but he did not give them his blessing and say that he would come back some time in the future. He did not suggest that they join the church although that is what they did later. He did not say that they should take part in rituals, and that would be sufficient. He did not suggest that their help to others was not enough and that they should do more and try harder.

What he did do was preach the gospel about Jesus.

He told them that Jesus is the Messiah and Lord of all. He told them that Jesus was the model of doing good and demonstrated compassion. Peter was with Jesus for three years. During such a length of time it is usually possible to find out people's strengths and weaknesses. Jesus was different; He had no cracks and flaws in His character. He spent His life for others. In spite of all our weaknesses flaws, foibles and failures, let us follow in the way of Jesus and seek to do good in this world.

Peter spoke to them about the death of Jesus. He referred to it by the cruel means of execution, by hanging on a tree, which Peter knew he himself would one day suffer. (John 21: 19)

Peter later wrote about the life and death of Jesus:

Who committed no sin, Nor was deceit found in His mouth"; who, when He was reviled, did not revile in return; when He suffered, He did not threaten, but committed Himself to Him who judges righteously; who Himself bore our sins in His own body on the tree, that we, having died to sins, might live for righteousness, by whose stripes you were healed. (1 Pet 2: 22-24)

Peter described how that after the resurrection Jesus appeared not to the people but to chosen witnesses, and how that the witnesses ate and drank with Him.Peter then went on to vindicate his hearers' fear of God by announcing that Jesus is our appointed judge. If we believe on Jesus, we will have forgiveness of sins. Peter was filled with the Holy Spirit as he uttered his sermon. The Holy Spirit fell upon the hearers, demonstrating that the gospel, from then on, was open to people from every part of the world, even to soldiers belonging to an army of occupation.

Let us never lose sight of the basics of Peter's message. Let us never cease to put Jesus at the centre of our witness.

It was after they had heard, and believed, and were saved, that they were then baptized.

Acts 11:1-18

1 Now the apostles and brethren who were in Judea heard that the Gentiles had also received the word of God. 2 And when Peter came up to Jerusalem, those of the circumcision contended with him, 3 saying, "You went in to uncircumcised men and ate with them!" 4 But Peter explained it to them in order from the beginning, saying: 5 "I was in the city of Joppa praying; and in a trance I saw a vision, an object descending like a great sheet, let down from heaven by four corners; and it came to me. 6 When I observed it intently and considered, I saw four-footed animals of the earth, wild beasts, creeping things, and birds of the air. 7 And I heard a voice saying to me, 'Rise, Peter; kill and eat.' 8 But I said, 'Not so, Lord! For nothing common or unclean has at any time entered my mouth.' 9 But the voice answered me again from heaven, 'What God has cleansed you must not call common.' 10 Now this was done three times, and all were drawn up again into heaven. 11 At that very moment, three men stood before the house where I was, having been sent to me from Caesarea. 12 Then the Spirit told me to go with them, doubting nothing. Moreover these six brethren accompanied me, and we entered the man's house. 13 And he told us how he had seen an angel standing in his house, who said to him, 'Send men to Joppa, and call for Simon whose surname is Peter, 14 who will tell you words by which you and all your household will be saved.' 15 And as I began to speak, the Holy Spirit fell upon them, as upon us at the beginning. 16 Then I remembered the word of the Lord, how He said, 'John indeed baptized with water, but you shall be baptized with the Holy Spirit.' 17 If therefore God gave them the same gift as He gave us when we believed on the Lord Jesus Christ, who was I that I could withstand God?" 18 When they heard these things they became silent; and they glorified God, saying, "Then God has also granted to the Gentiles repentance to life.

There is good teaching and advice for us in this passage. The first thing to note is the great patience of God in His dealings with His people. The account of Peter's vision is told again. It contained a message that took much persistence to sink in. There is no doubt Luke made great efforts to make the point that Gentiles could become fully part of God's people without becoming Jewish.

They were to be totally integrated into the faith. Not only did Peter find it difficult to take this on board, so did other believers. Rumour and gossip spread quickly around the churches, and as one would expect, the news of Peter's ministry to the Gentiles was accompanied with great puzzlement and unease. Peter came to learn to be patient by the example of Jesus and through the Holy Spirit, since patience is one of the fruits of the Spirit. (Gal 5:22) 2 Peter describes the patience of God towards those who are slow in coming to faith. "The Lord is not slack concerning His promise, as some count slackness, but is longsuffering toward us, not willing that any should perish but that all should come to repentance." (2 Pet 3: 9) If God is patient or "longsuffering",then so should we.. There has been too much distress in the world caused by lack of patience.

The second thing to note is the way Peter dealt with the news of salvation to the Gentiles and his part in it. He could have been rigid and said that he was an apostle and that is the way it is; no arguments, no more questions! Instead, he was totally transparent and open in his explanation. He described the vision. He described the sermon to Cornelius and his friends. He described the way in which the Holy Spirit fell on his hearers. He then put Jesus at the centre by quoting His teaching on the matter, "John truly baptized with water but you will be baptized with the Holy Spirit.`` (Acts 1: 5)

This openness and explanation brought his hearers on board with these new developments. They had understood, and their long-held stubborn mind-set of complete separation from Gentiles began to change, and they praised God for what had happened.

Leaders in the church, and indeed all walks of life, would do well to follow Peter's example and give full explanations for their actions and policies. Many a church and organization has been brought into division by autocratic leadership and a lack of sharing and openness.

One final note on this passage is what was not said, but became evident in the epistles. Although Peter's hearers were thrilled and were delighted that, "God had granted the Gentiles repentance to life," (v 18) there remained a significant number of Jews who would later hamper gospel ministry by insisting that new believers should take on Jewish customs and rituals, in particular circumcision. This teaching was a great hindrance to the growth of the church to such an extent that it was also a denial of the gospel. Not long after, the apostle Paul wrote this:

As we have said before, so now I say again, if anyone preaches any other gospel to you than what you have received, let him be accursed. (Gal 1: 9)

It is therefore not surprising that a significantly long section of Acts is concerned with what was to be a continuing, disruptive and crucial issue. Let us never forget that we are not saved by attending rituals, or adopting a certain lifestyle, or by joining a particular church, important as they may be. We are saved by faith in Christ. Such saving faith leads to a willing and obedient heart. Peter believed and taught that, so did Paul and John and all the other New Testament writers, and so should we.

Acts 11:19-30

19 Now those who were scattered after the persecution that arose over Stephen traveled as far as Phoenicia, Cyprus, and Antioch, preaching the word to no one but the Jews only. **20** But some of them were men from Cyprus and Cyrene, who, when they had come to Antioch, spoke to the Hellenists, preaching the Lord Jesus. **21** And the hand of the Lord was with them, and a great number believed and turned to the Lord. **22** Then news of these things came to the ears of the church in Jerusalem, and they sent out Barnabas to go as far as Antioch. **23** When he came and had seen the grace of God, he was glad, and encouraged them all that with purpose of heart they should continue with the Lord. **24** For he was a good man, full of the Holy Spirit and of faith. And a great many people were added to the Lord. **25** Then Barnabas departed for Tarsus to seek Saul. **26** And when he had found him, he brought him to Antioch. So it was that for a whole year they assembled with the church and taught a great many people. And the disciples were first called Christians in Antioch. **27** And in these days prophets came from Jerusalem to Antioch. **28** Then one of them, named Agabus, stood up and showed by the Spirit that there was going to be a great famine throughout all the world, which also happened in the days of Claudius Caesar. **29** Then the disciples, each according to his ability, determined to send relief to the brethren dwelling in Judea. **30** This they also did, and sent it to the elders by the hands of Barnabas and Saul.

This passage describes in a few sentences the beginning of a church-plant in one of the most important cities of the Roman Empire. It began as a consequence of persecution, when believers fled from Jerusalem and the surrounding area, to places and cities far and wide. One of those cities was Antioch, which was hundreds of kilometres north of Jerusalem. Although they were fleeing persecution, they still spoke about Jesus. Then another important development took place. We do not know if they were aware of Peter's vision and ministry to Gentiles. The news may have travelled very rapidly, even to Cyprus and North Africa. Believers from those parts began to evangelize amongst the Gentiles in Antioch.

We do not know the names of these evangelists. They are not celebrated in the history of the church, but the work they did was of tremendous consequence, and, more importantly, the "hand of the Lord was with them". (v 21) We may never know the significance of what we do in our lives. Very, very few are remembered in the history books. God knows, and the crucial thing is to be in His book of life, and to have His hand on our lives. Many politicians and famous people want to make their mark in history, but our ambition should be to make our mark for God.

News of what was happening in Antioch soon reached Jerusalem and the apostles sent just the right man to investigate. Barnabas was from Cyprus as were the original evangelists to the Gentiles of Antioch. As has already been noted, he was a 'people person', a man who invested in the kingdom of God. He put Jesus first in his life. In this passage we also note that he had the stamina, courage and willingness to travel long distances for the sake of the spread of the gospel.

Here we also note his gift as a speaker and teacher. It would be a tremendous benefit to the advancement of the church of God, if more people were noted to be "full of the Holy Spirit and of faith." (v 24)

Although Saul was a controversial figure because of his past history, Barnabas made a big effort to seek him out. The growing church in Antioch needed a man of Saul's gifts to be able to continue the ministry there.

The verses, which describe the prophecy of Agabus, are fascinating. It was accurate and the disciples were obedient to the consequences of famine and provided money and gifts for the "brethren dwelling in Judaea". (v 29) Although God sometimes makes His intention clear today in a similar way, many make predictions which later prove to be inaccurate and therefore any modern claims should be treated with great caution. However, Agabus was both clear and accurate. Paul later stated that God's household, that is, the church is built on the foundation of the apostles and prophets, with Christ Himself as the chief cornerstone (Eph 2: 20)

We do not know much about these early prophets but no doubt many of them were travelling preachers, who endured great hardship and suffering.

Finally, the word 'Christian' is used for the first time in Antioch. Since then, the term has been used as abuse as well as description. We who are called Christians should never be ashamed of the label and always be willing to identify ourselves with the cause and sufferings of Christ.

Acts 12:1-25

1 Now about that time Herod the king stretched out his hand to harass some from the church. 2 Then he killed James the brother of John with the sword. 3 And because he saw that it pleased the Jews, he proceeded further to seize Peter also. Now it was during the Days of Unleavened Bread. 4 So when he had arrested him, he put him in prison, and delivered him to four squads of soldiers to keep him, intending to bring him before the people after Passover. 5 Peter was therefore kept in prison, but constant prayer was offered to God for him by the church. 6 And when Herod was about to bring him out, that night Peter was sleeping, bound with two chains between two soldiers; and the guards before the door were keeping the prison. 7 Now behold, an angel of the Lord stood by him, and a light shone in the prison; and he struck Peter on the side and raised him up, saying, "Arise quickly!" And his chains fell off his hands. 8 Then the angel said to him, "Gird yourself and tie on your sandals"; and so he did. And he said to him, "Put on your garment and follow me." 9 So he went out and followed him, and did not know that what was done by the angel was real, but thought he was seeing a vision. 10 When they were past the first and the second guard posts, they came to the iron gate that leads to the city, which opened to them of its own accord; and they went out and went down one street, and immediately the angel departed from him. 11 And when Peter had come to himself, he said, "Now I know for certain that the Lord has sent His angel, and has delivered me from the hand of Herod and from all the expectation of the Jewish people." 12 So, when he had considered this, he came to the house of Mary, the mother of John whose surname was Mark, where many were gathered together praying. 13 And as Peter knocked at the door of the gate, a girl named Rhoda came to answer. 14 When she recognized Peter's voice, because of her gladness she did not open the gate, but ran in and announced that Peter stood before the gate. 15 But they said to her, "You are beside yourself!" Yet she kept insisting that it was so. So they said, "It is his angel." 16 Now Peter continued knocking; and when they opened the door and saw him, they were astonished. 17 But motioning to them with his hand to keep silent, he declared to them how the Lord had brought him out of the prison. And he said, "Go, tell these things to James and to the brethren." And he departed and went to another place. 18 Then, as soon as it was day, there was no small stir among the soldiers about what had become of Peter. 19 But when Herod had searched for

him and not found him, he examined the guards and commanded that they should be put to death. And he went down from Judea to Caesarea, and stayed there. **20** Now Herod had been very angry with the people of Tyre and Sidon; but they came to him with one accord, and having made Blastus the king's personal aide their friend, they asked for peace, because their country was supplied with food by the king's country. **21** So on a set day Herod, arrayed in royal apparel, sat on his throne and gave an oration to them. **22** And the people kept shouting, "The voice of a god and not of a man!" **23** Then immediately an angel of the Lord struck him, because he did not give glory to God. And he was eaten by worms and died. **24** But the word of God grew and multiplied. **25** And Barnabas and Saul returned from Jerusalem when they had fulfilled their ministry, and they also took with them John whose surname was Mark.

The arrest of James, the brother of John, with other believers began a new phase of persecution. This time it is at the hands of King Herod Agrippa I, who was a grandson of Herod the Great, who, in turn, was king at the time of the birth of Jesus. These men tried to placate the Jewish leadership, but cared little about God. The problem Herod perceived was that these Christians honoured and worshiped another king, Jesus, and therefore were considered a threat. Although we assert that Jesus' kingdom is not of this world, secular tyrants like Herod were and are always uneasy when it comes to Christianity.

The first question we might ask is why did God allow James to be beheaded, whilst Peter was freed? We cannot know why, but we do know that James went to be with his Lord. Secondly, as with many other Christian martyrs, it cannot be doubted that James received special comfort and presence from God in order to face his ordeal. Subsequently, all the apostles endured persecution, and nearly all suffered a violent death.

In recent times, many Christians have died at the hands of those who seek to resist God. Those who put themselves against God will ultimately fail. God's purposes will never be overcome. Although many have tried to ignore, resist, or pit themselves against God, they end in eventual failure. There are many Christians who feel that they are on the losing side, they feel weak and are small in number, but Jesus wins, and will win in the end. All the prophecies about Jesus have been and will be fulfilled. All His promises have and will come true.

Building on his apparent success, Herod arrested Peter. In order to ensure the timing, the wily ruler kept Peter in prison until all the noise and bustle of the Passover and the feast of unleavened bread were over, and the crowds had left Jerusalem. Peter was kept in chains and under a round-the-clock guard. Peter knew that he would soon be under the sentence of death. If anyone had cause to have a sleepless or restless night, it was Peter. He was in a daze as the angel led him out of the cells and into the street. God can do things for us and solve problems before we have stirred and realize what has happened.

Many have tried to deny the truth of Scripture and assert that most of the narrative is a devised fable, but who would have devised the story of Rhoda and Peter's continued knocking on the door? (v 16) With all the seriousness of Scripture and the grave danger that disciples faced, there was still room for some humour.

It was commendable that everyone had assembled for a long, earnest prayer meeting. It reveals their human nature when they refused to believe that their prayer had been answered until the door had been opened and Peter walked in. There are some who have much zeal but limited faith. We should ask God to increase our faith, reliance, and trust in Him.

The demise of Herod recorded at the end of the Chapter is also recorded elsewhere in the writings of the Jewish historian, Josephus. The point Luke makes is that unlike Peter who refused veneration and worship, Herod accepted it. His death is used to prove that opposition to God, or acceptance of worship is, in the end, futile, and may be lethal.

Acts 13:1-5

1 Now in the church that was at Antioch there were certain prophets and teachers: Barnabas, Simeon who was called Niger, Lucius of Cyrene, Manaen who had been brought up with Herod the tetrarch, and Saul. 2 As they ministered to the Lord and fasted, the Holy Spirit said, "Now separate to Me Barnabas and Saul for the work to which I have called them." 3 Then, having fasted and prayed, and laid hands on them, they sent them away. 4 So, being sent out by the Holy Spirit, they went down to Seleucia, and from there they sailed to Cyprus. 5 And when they arrived in Salamis, they preached the word of God in the synagogues of the Jews. They also had John as their assistant.

The named leaders of the church in Antioch were of varied backgrounds and experiences, but they were one in fellowship. It is a wonderful thing about the church of God that it brings people together of different origins and ability who would not normally meet each other socially. But in God's kingdom, they love one another, work together and pray together. Happy is the church where social and cultural divisions have been broken down. (Eph 1: 10)

Conversely, those churches where social privilege persists become the ones that lose their effectiveness. In Antioch they prayed and fasted together. It was a praying, fasting, teaching, growing and sending church. It remains a model for subsequent generations.

The prayer which Jesus taught us, or "The Lord's Prayer", is a wonderful model which we do not consider enough. (Luke 11:2-4) The aspect of the prayer, which was being activated here was, "Thy kingdom come. Thy will be done." The first part is demonstrated by the desire to spread the gospel and extend God's kingdom. The second part was to do God's will, by the choice of Barnabas and Saul. They were to be the human agency to carry out the missionary enterprise. Saul wrote later that the whole creation has been groaning, and waiting for the redemption of our bodies. (Rom 8: 22-23) We should always have a concern for those who have never heard the Gospel.

Barnabas and Saul were just the right people. They had natural gifts. They understood the culture of the places to be visited. They were mentally tough and would not be put off by opposition and persecution. They were physically strong and able to endure hardship and privation. However, the most important feature was that they were called by God and filled with the Holy Spirit for the work they were about to do. Every decision of this nature and seriousness was begun and ended with prayer. The church was an unselfish church in that they were prepared to commission two of their most gifted leaders and preachers and send them out.

The mission began in earnest when Barnabas, Saul and John Mark landed in Eastern Cyprus. Cyprus already had some believing residents, since some of the initial evangelists to Antioch were from that island. The primary effort was to the Jewish synagogues. It is a fact of history that in the first years of the Christian church, the predominant number of believers was Jewish. After that beginning, the majority were Gentiles, with very few Jews. It has remained that way for two thousand years. Initially, as we have already noted, Jews persecuted Christians. Afterwards, so-called Christian Gentiles persecuted Jews. It remains a terrible stain on the history of the church. The fascinating thing is that there are more Jewish Christians or Messianic believers, as they prefer to be called, today, than at any other time since the first century. It was one of Paul's greatest heartaches that the vast majority of Jews had rejected Jesus, their Messiah. A significant part of his epistle to the Romans is dedicated to that particular issue. He wrote:

For I speak to you Gentiles; inasmuch as I am an apostle to the Gentiles, I magnify my ministry, if by any means I may provoke to jealousy those who are my flesh and save some of them. For if their being cast away is the reconciling of the world, what will their acceptance be but life from the dead? (Rom 11: 13-15)

There should always be a space in our thinking and prayers for the Jewish people, for, "They are beloved for the sake of the fathers." (Rom 11: 28)

Acts 13:6-12

6 Now when they had gone through the island to Paphos, they found a certain sorcerer, a false prophet, a Jew whose name was Bar-Jesus, 7 who was with the proconsul, Sergius Paulus, an intelligent man. This man called for Barnabas and Saul and sought to hear the word of God. 8 But Elymas the sorcerer (for so his name is translated) withstood them, seeking to turn the proconsul away from the faith. 9 Then Saul, who also is called Paul, filled with the Holy Spirit, looked intently at him 10 and said, "O full of all deceit and all fraud, you son of the devil, you enemy of all righteousness, will you not cease perverting the straight ways of the Lord? 11 And now, indeed, the hand of the Lord is upon you, and you shall be blind, not seeing the sun for a time." And immediately a dark mist fell on him, and he went around seeking someone to lead him by the hand. 12 Then the proconsul believed, when he saw what had been done, being astonished at the teaching of the Lord.

The ancient world was full of magicians, astrologers and sorcerers, who plied their trade on the vulnerable and gullible. Not only were the gullible deceived, but also all the rulers and governors had their own soothsayers in residence. Such superstitions have persisted till modern times. Some of the most respected political leaders and their wives have consulted their own gurus and astrologers. Newspapers and magazines are full of horoscopes and "mystic advice". It seems that the most unbelieving generation is also the most superstitious. As noted earlier, these fortune-tellers are at best dangerous nonsense, at worst, a satanic invention. The Bible advises us to keep well away from these damaging distractions. "Resist the devil, and he will flee from you." (James 4: 7)

Simon the sorcerer gave the impression that he had become a true believer. The magician, Elymas, gave no such impression. He opposed from the start. The devil will use any ploy to frustrate the mission of God.

Elymas, the sorcerer in residence, urged Sergius Paulus, the Roman proconsul, to ignore the word of God. Today, although they may not be sorcerers, there are plenty of journalists and media personalities who urge us to put Christ aside and ignore the Bible.

The intervention of Paul reminds us, as we have already noted, that opposition to God's work is ultimately futile. We know that Paul's blindness was temporary and during that period of blindness he prayed and continued to commit his life to Christ. We are not told whether this sorcerer became a believer or not. Were his eyes opened, or did he remain faithless and permanently blind? We can only assume that he remained unconverted.

The conversion of Sergius Paulus reminds us that there are a few people of ability and high rank who become believers. If we are in any position of influence we should do all that we can to commend Christ and contribute generously to the work of God. God so frequently uses the ordinary people to do big things for Him. Occasionally, he uses the privileged. In his first letter to the Corinthians, Paul made the following observation:

For you see your calling, brethren, that not many wise according to the flesh, not many mighty, not many noble, are called. But God has chosen the foolish things of the world to put to shame the wise, and God has chosen the weak things of the world to put to shame the things which are mighty; and the base things of the world and the things which are despised God has chosen, and the things which are not, to bring to nothing the things that are, that no flesh should glory in His presence. (1 Cor 1: 26-29)

The important thing is that mission is God's work, and no matter what natural abilities we may have, important as they are, it can only truly succeed when done by the inspiration and power of the Holy Spirit.

Sergius Paulus was the first Gentile convert named in Acts who was neither a proselyte nor a God-fearing Greek. It was a further transcultural step that the three missionaries had to take. Perhaps, Paul was the one who was able to make that transition the most readily, for he declared, "I have become all things to all men, that I might by all means save some." (1 Cor 9: 22)

Acts 13:13-52

13 Now when Paul and his party set sail from Paphos, they came to Perga in Pamphylia; and John, departing from them, returned to Jerusalem. 14 But when they departed from Perga, they came to Antioch in Pisidia, and went into the synagogue on the Sabbath day and sat down. 15 And after the reading of the Law and the Prophets, the rulers of the synagogue sent to them, saying, "Men and brethren, if you have any word of exhortation for the people, say on." 16 Then Paul stood up, and motioning with his hand said, "Men of Israel, and you who fear God, listen: 17 The God of this people Israel chose our fathers, and exalted the people when they dwelt as strangers in the land of Egypt, and with an uplifted arm He brought them out of it. 18 Now for a time of about forty years He put up with their ways in the wilderness. 19 And when He had destroyed seven nations in the land of Canaan, He distributed their land to them by allotment. 20 After that He gave them judges for about four hundred and fifty years, until Samuel the prophet. 21 And afterward they asked for a king; so God gave them Saul the son of Kish, a man of the tribe of Benjamin, for forty years. 22 And when He had removed him, He raised up for them David as king, to whom also He gave testimony and said, 'I have found David the son of Jesse, a man after My own heart, who will do all My will.' 23 From this man's seed, according to the promise, God raised up for Israel a Saviour Jesus 24 after John had first preached, before His coming, the baptism of repentance to all the people of Israel. 25 And as John was finishing his course, he said, 'Who do you think I am? I am not He. But behold, there comes One after me, the sandals of whose feet I am not worthy to loose.' 26 Men and brethren, sons of the family of Abraham, and those among you who fear God, to you the word of this salvation has been sent. 27 For those who dwell in Jerusalem, and their rulers, because they did not know Him, nor even the voices of the Prophets which are read every Sabbath, have fulfilled them in condemning Him. 28 And though they found no cause for death in Him, they asked Pilate that He should be put to death. 29 Now when they had fulfilled all that was written concerning Him, they took Him down from the tree and laid Him in a tomb. 30 But God raised Him from the dead. 31 He was seen for many days by those who came up with Him from Galilee to Jerusalem, who are His witnesses to the people. 32 And we declare to you glad tidings--that promise which was made to the fathers. 33 God has fulfilled this for us their children,

in that He has raised up Jesus. As it is also written in the second Psalm: 'You are My Son, Today I have begotten You.' **34** And that He raised Him from the dead, no more to return to corruption, He has spoken thus: 'I will give you the sure mercies of David.' **35** Therefore He also says in another Psalm: 'You will not allow Your Holy One to see corruption.' **36** "For David, after he had served his own generation by the will of God, fell asleep, was buried with his fathers, and saw corruption; **37** but He whom God raised up saw no corruption. **38** Therefore let it be known to you, brethren, that through this Man is preached to you the forgiveness of sins; **39** and by Him everyone who believes is justified from all things from which you could not be justified by the law of Moses. **40** Beware therefore, lest what has been spoken in the prophets come upon you: **41** Behold, you despisers, Marvel and perish! For I work a work in your days, A work which you will by no means believe, Though one were to declare it to you. **42** So when the Jews went out of the synagogue, the Gentiles begged that these words might be preached to them the next Sabbath. **43** Now when the congregation had broken up, many of the Jews and devout proselytes followed Paul and Barnabas, who, speaking to them, persuaded them to continue in the grace of God. **44** On the next Sabbath almost the whole city came together to hear the word of God. **45** But when the Jews saw the multitudes, they were filled with envy; and contradicting and blaspheming, they opposed the things spoken by Paul. **46** Then Paul and Barnabas grew bold and said, "It was necessary that the word of God should be spoken to you first; but since you reject it, and judge yourselves unworthy of everlasting life, behold, we turn to the Gentiles. **47** For so the Lord has commanded us: 'I have set you as a light to the Gentiles, That you should be for salvation to the ends of the earth.' " **48** Now when the Gentiles heard this, they were glad and glorified the word of the Lord. And as many as had been appointed to eternal life believed. **49** And the word of the Lord was being spread throughout all the region. **50** But the Jews stirred up the devout and prominent women and the chief men of the city, raised up persecution against Paul and Barnabas, and expelled them from their region. **51** But they shook off the dust from their feet against them, and came to Iconium. **52** And the disciples were filled with joy and with the Holy Spirit.

From Cyprus, the missionaries sailed to Pamphylia, which is on the southern part of modern Turkey. We do not know why John Mark left them but it was to be a cause of friction and frustration. It could have been for one or several of the reasons why Christians leave their place of work or activity. It could have been that Mark was afraid of the likely dangers in the mountains that would be encountered on the journey to the next city. The road was probably unsafe, the terrain was hazardous and the hills inhabited by robbers.

It could be that he had burnout and had had enough. Again, this was and is not unusual in Christian ministry.

It may have been that the thought of mixing more freely than ever in a pagan culture to spread and share the gospel was a step too far and outside his comfort zone. In other words, he was unable to cross the cultural divide between Jewish and pagan cultures. Some or all of these issues may have contributed to John Mark's departure. These issues of cultural differences remain relevant to this day.

In spite of this setback, and after the other apparent setbacks in Acts, the work still went on. It is comforting to know that in spite of all our weaknesses and failures, the gospel advances. Although this is reassuring, it should not mean that it is acceptable to be lazy, or fail to respond to God's call. So often the reply is, "Here am I, please send someone else."

On arrival at the synagogue in Pisidia Antioch, Saul has become Paul, and he has also become the lead speaker. Perhaps, even Barnabas was having some difficulty with the culture change.

Paul's sermon was notable for the similarity to those of Peter and Stephen. He began on the same ground as his hearers. He reminded them how God had blessed them in the history of Israel. He spoke about their freedom from slavery, and how God guided them through the judges and prophets. It was God who had given them a king, David, who was a man after God's own heart. (1 Sam 13: 14) Those who preach would be prudent to try to begin alongside the hearers and bring them step-by-step to where God wants them to be.

We should note Paul's use of the Old Testament. It is a tragedy that some Christians today relegate the Old Testament to a low place in their estimation. It too is part of God's revealed word and should be given the same respect that Jesus and the New Testament writers gave it. We should read the Hebrew Scriptures through a New Testament "lens", but we should never forget that there is a single strand of God's redeeming purpose running through the whole Bible, and that the New Testament is a fulfilment of the Old.

Paul ended his sermon with Jesus, His death and resurrection, and that salvation and forgiveness of sins was through faith in Him. He warned them of future judgement. Jesus, the apostles, and faithful preachers during the long and varied history of the church have never neglected to preach about judgement and neither should we. These themes should always be at the forefront of our Christian understanding. The church has always been an engine of social change, and the improvement of people's lives. However, Paul's primary task was to preach the gospel to everyone, whatever their need or background.

Paul knew the Scriptures intimately. He probably could recite the Old Testament off by heart. We should make every effort to read the Bible regularly, and at the end of each year ask ourselves the question. "Do I know my Bible better than I did last January?"

The expulsion of Paul and Barnabas from the region shows the extent of opposition that gospel ministry can receive. Some of the most vocal against the gospel are those who consider themselves to be religious. Nevertheless, there were many Jews, God-fearing Gentiles and other Gentiles who 'just happened' to be interested, who became believers. As in other places in Acts, they were transformed with joy in spite of the surrounding turmoil.

Acts 14:1-20

Now it happened in Iconium that they went together to the synagogue of the Jews, and so spoke that a great multitude both of the Jews and of the Greeks believed. **2** But the unbelieving Jews stirred up the Gentiles and poisoned their minds against the brethren. **3** Therefore they stayed there a long time, speaking boldly in the Lord, who was bearing witness to the word of His grace, granting signs and wonders to be done by their hands. **4** But the multitude of the city was divided: part sided with the Jews, and part with the apostles. **5** And when a violent attempt was made by both the Gentiles and Jews, with their rulers, to abuse and stone them, **6** they became aware of it and fled to Lystra and Derbe, cities of Lycaonia, and to the surrounding region. **7** And they were preaching the gospel there. **8** And in Lystra a certain man without strength in his feet was sitting, a cripple from his mother's womb, who had never walked. **9** This man heard Paul speaking. Paul, observing him intently and seeing that he had faith to be healed, **10** said with a loud voice, "Stand up straight on your feet!" And he leaped and walked. **11** Now when the people saw what Paul had done, they raised their voices, saying in the Lycaonian language, "The gods have come down to us in the likeness of men!" **12** And Barnabas they called Zeus, and Paul, Hermes, because he was the chief speaker. **13** Then the priest of Zeus, whose temple was in front of their city, brought oxen and garlands to the gates, intending to sacrifice with the multitudes. **14** But when the apostles Barnabas and Paul heard this, they tore their clothes and ran in among the multitude, crying out **15** and saying, "Men, why are you doing these things? We also are men with the same nature as you, and preach to you that you should turn from these useless things to the living God, who made the heaven, the earth, the sea, and all things that are in them, **16** who in bygone generations allowed all nations to walk in their own ways. **17** Nevertheless He did not leave Himself without witness, in that He did good, gave us rain from heaven and fruitful seasons, filling our hearts with food and gladness." **18** And with these sayings they could scarcely restrain the multitudes from sacrificing to them. **19** Then Jews from Antioch and Iconium came there; and having persuaded the multitudes, they stoned Paul and dragged him out of the city, supposing him to be dead. **20** However, when the disciples gathered around him, he rose up and went into the city. And the next day he departed with Barnabas to Derbe.

At Iconium, a great number of both Jews and Gentiles believed. Paul and Barnabas were able to stay there for a number of weeks. In that place, they taught, and God confirmed the message through signs and wonders. Then the opposition began.

We learn a few important points here.

Firstly, in spite of the kind and gracious words, there were people who hated the message. Moreover they provoked and urged others against the message. This phenomenon has become increasingly common in the West where new atheists stir up opposition to Christianity through their writings and the media. We are told directly and by implication that modern, educated and urbane people have no further reason to believe in God, Christ or the gospel.

Secondly, the wonderful way people were helped, and no doubt healed through the signs and miracles, was greeted with resistance. It remains surprising that those who oppose the gospel to this day wilfully ignore the pioneering roles and work that Christians have done in education, healthcare, care of the dying, social reform, slavery abolition, third world medicine and the like.

Thirdly, those who were divided, sometimes by mutual hatred, came together to persecute Paul and Barnabas. A similar thing happened when Pharisees, Sadducees and the Herodians conspired against Jesus. (Matt 22: 15-23) Those who were divided and loathed each other became united in their hatred of Christ.

In spite of all this, Paul and Barnabas were undaunted in the task that God had called them to do. Many became believers and were hungry to learn more about their newfound faith. Many of us retreat at the first hint of resistance. We need to pray for the wisdom and grace to know when to stand, when to ignore, when to contend and when to withdraw. Whatever happens, a true witness for Christ will never please everyone. When the lives of Paul and Barnabas were at risk, they moved on, only to make a quiet visit later.

The events at Lystra moved on as rapidly as they were surprising.

Paul and Barnabas arrived as travelling preachers and were given a hearing by a sizeable crowd. Preachers are frequently able to discern from looking at the congregation's body language what is going on. Some are smiling, attentive and eager to hear God's word. Some appear sleepy and bored. Others look mistrusting and suspicious, whilst with many, there is no idea what is going on. One of Paul's congregation was "lame from birth", but he was all eyes and ears. He wanted a new start in life and Paul could see that the man was taking everything on board. However, Paul had some extra God-inspired discernment and saw that the man had the faith to be healed. God, following Paul's call to, "Stand up", healed the man! He was ready for a new start spiritually, and ready to take on the role and responsibility of being able-bodied.

The crowd's reaction to this healing was remarkable and difficult for modern people to understand. The people of Lystra had a legend that the ancient gods, Zeus and Hermes would one day visit their city, and it was their responsibility to recognize it. This healing sparked a mass reaction, and Barnabas who was the more imposing figure was named as Zeus whilst Paul, the smaller lead speaker was Hermes. Paul and Barnabas had to prevent sacrifices being made to them. At least, they had a chance to address the crowd. The content of the message was quite different from that given to a Jewish audience. Paul tried to throw overboard the idea of a multiplicity of gods and explain the evidence for one God by the blessings given at His hand. The presence of creation itself is sufficient evidence for the existence of God.

Later Paul wrote to the Romans:

For since the creation of the world His invisible attributes are clearly seen, being understood by the things that are made, even His eternal power and Godhead, so that they are without excuse. (Rom 1: 20)

Paul's reasoning was countered by the presence of Jews who managed to win over the crowd. The fickle nature of humanity was demonstrated by the change of attitude towards Paul, from regarding him as a god to a hated criminal in the space of a few hours or even minutes. The stoning of Paul was a cruel act of mob violence. He was comforted by God who drew close to him as he later described to the Corinthians. (2 Cor 12: 2-4) Brave converts surrounded him, and helped him back into the city. We need to identify and stand with all Christians in all parts of the world who suffer for their faith whatever the risk and inconvenience to ourselves.

Remember the prisoners as if chained with them, those who are mistreated, since you yourselves are in the body also. (Heb 13: 3)

Acts 14:20-15:2

20 However, when the disciples gathered around him, he rose up and went into the city. And the next day he departed with Barnabas to Derbe. **21** And when they had preached the gospel to that city and made many disciples, they returned to Lystra, Iconium, and Antioch, **22** strengthening the souls of the disciples, exhorting them to continue in the faith, and saying, "We must through many tribulations enter the kingdom of God." **23** So when they had appointed elders in every church, and prayed with fasting, they commended them to the Lord in whom they had believed. **24** And after they had passed through Pisidia, they came to Pamphylia. **25** Now when they had preached the word in Perga, they went down to Attalia. **26** From there they sailed to Antioch, where they had been commended to the grace of God for the work which they had completed. **27** Now when they had come and gathered the church together, they reported all that God had done with them, and that He had opened the door of faith to the Gentiles. **28** So they stayed there a long time with the disciples.

1 And certain men came down from Judea and taught the brethren, "Unless you are circumcised according to the custom of Moses, you cannot be saved." **2** Therefore, when Paul and Barnabas had no small dissension and dispute with them, they determined that Paul and Barnabas and certain others of them should go up to Jerusalem, to the apostles and elders, about this question.

In Derbe, Paul and Barnabas continued preaching and experienced a respite from persecution. I think we can say that the two missionaries received more physical punishment during this journey than is described here in Acts. Later Paul stated that he bore on his body the marks of the Lord Jesus. (Gal 6:17) The covert return to the cities of Lystra, Iconium and Antioch reassured Paul and Barnabas that the converts were standing firm in the faith. It also demonstrated the extraordinary bravery of these two servants of Christ.

When they explained that we must go through many hardships

to enter the kingdom of God, they said something very relevant to our age. Sometimes, Christ is presented as a great fulfilment, the solution to our problems, or even a 'feel good' experience, but few appreciate that there is a cross as well as a crown. Yes, there is joy that had not been experienced before, a meaning and purpose not previously known, and sometimes an overwhelming sense of the love of God. However, Christians too have to face hardship, illness, disappointment and distress. On top of that, there may be trials of varying degrees of hostility from others around us.

Their return to the missionary-sending church in Syrian Antioch allowed them to recover from their hardships. All servants of Christ need times of rest and recuperation before returning to the places of trial and persecution.

Whilst at Antioch, an internal church problem, which had already been around for some time, erupted. Upon the outcome of the ensuing debate, hung the future of Christianity. Was it to become a continuation as a Jewish sect, or a worldwide movement? The issues seemed minor, the need for a surgical operation, circumcision, and observance of some legalities, but the issues were in fact major - was salvation to be through faith alone?We learn some important lessons from this dispute, which on the surface appears to be about trivial points of doctrine.

Firstly, we see the necessity to be clear on the requirements for salvation, and if necessary contend even with our fellow Christians. The issue of doctrine and what we believe is of profound importance.

Secondly, it is understandable that lifelong Jews who had become believers in Christ should wish to hang on to the law and their traditions. After all, although Jesus was critical of the hypocrisy and ridiculous practices of the Jewish leadership, he lived as a Jew.

It is easy to understand the reasoning that some may have used, "It is all very well opening the door to Samaritans and people like Cornelius, but announcing the good news in the streets of pagan towns and taking on people who have no background of religious understanding is just too far. They have to become like us."

Paul and Barnabas' view was that we all are unable to keep the whole law, anyway, and that we all have to come to Christ by faith and this is what saves us. Works are evidence and proof of our faith and it is right to lead godly lives, attend worship, study the Scriptures, but these things in themselves do not save us!

Thirdly, an insistence on faith and works for salvation is found in so many quarters. Muslims, for example, state that the Qu'ran teaches the necessity of both faith and good works: "To those who believe and do deeds of righteousness hath Allah promised forgiveness and great reward." (Qu'ran 5:9)

The Roman Catholic Church, and other forms of Catholicism say that grace and salvation are mediated by a priesthood, through the sacraments, and that believers should of necessity join the Catholic Church. Although both Popes Benedict and Francis have in recent years tried to bridge the gap between the Catholic Church and Luther, (Catholic Answers Magazine, Vol. 20 No. 7), contemporary Catholic writings remain critical of Protestant interpretation of the means of salvation, to the extent of calling it, and those who teach it, 'anathema'. (Christian Apologetics and Research Ministry)

There are all kinds of people who add "musts" to grace. We all have a tendency to do it. All these may seem on the surface, insignificant points, but they affect very profoundly the way we present the gospel.

Acts 15:3-35

3 So, being sent on their way by the church, they passed through Phoenicia and Samaria, describing the conversion of the Gentiles; and they caused great joy to all the brethren. 4 And when they had come to Jerusalem, they were received by the church and the apostles and the elders; and they reported all things that God had done with them. 5 But some of the sect of the Pharisees who believed rose up, saying, "It is necessary to circumcise them, and to command them to keep the law of Moses." 6 Now the apostles and elders came together to consider this matter. 7 And when there had been much dispute, Peter rose up and said to them: "Men and brethren, you know that a good while ago God chose among us, that by my mouth the Gentiles should hear the word of the gospel and believe. 8 So God, who knows the heart, acknowledged them by giving them the Holy Spirit, just as He did to us, 9 and made no distinction between us and them, purifying their hearts by faith. 10 Now therefore, why do you test God by putting a yoke on the neck of the disciples which neither our fathers nor we were able to bear? 11 But we believe that through the grace of the Lord Jesus Christ we shall be saved in the same manner as they." 12 Then all the multitude kept silent and listened to Barnabas and Paul declaring how many miracles and wonders God had worked through them among the Gentiles. 13 And after they had become silent, James answered, saying, "Men and brethren, listen to me: 14 Simon has declared how God at the first visited the Gentiles to take out of them a people for His name. 15 And with this the words of the prophets agree, just as it is written: 16 'After this I will return And will rebuild the tabernacle of David, which has fallen down; I will rebuild its ruins, And I will set it up; 17 So that the rest of mankind may seek the Lord, Even all the Gentiles who are called by My name, Says the Lord who does all these things.' 18 "Known to God from eternity are all His works. 19 Therefore I judge that we should not trouble those from among the Gentiles who are turning to God, 20 but that we write to them to abstain from things polluted by idols, from sexual immorality, from things strangled, and from blood. 21 For Moses has had throughout many generations those who preach him in every city, being read in the synagogues every Sabbath." 22 Then it pleased the apostles and elders, with the whole church, to send chosen men of their own company to Antioch with Paul and Barnabas, namely, Judas who was also named Barsabas, and Silas, leading men among the brethren. 23 They wrote this letter by them: The apostles, the elders, and

the brethren, To the brethren who are of the Gentiles in Antioch, Syria, and Cilicia: Greetings. 24 Since we have heard that some who went out from us have troubled you with words, unsettling your souls, saying, "You must be circumcised and keep the law"--to whom we gave no such commandment-- 25 it seemed good to us, being assembled with one accord, to send chosen men to you with our beloved Barnabas and Paul, 26 men who have risked their lives for the name of our Lord Jesus Christ. 27 We have therefore sent Judas and Silas, who will also report the same things by word of mouth. 28 For it seemed good to the Holy Spirit, and to us, to lay upon you no greater burden than these necessary things: 29 that you abstain from things offered to idols, from blood, from things strangled, and from sexual immorality. If you keep yourselves from these, you will do well. Farewell. 30 So when they were sent off, they came to Antioch; and when they had gathered the multitude together, they delivered the letter. 31 When they had read it, they rejoiced over its encouragement. 32 Now Judas and Silas, themselves being prophets also, exhorted and strengthened the brethren with many words. 33 And after they had stayed there for a time, they were sent back with greetings from the brethren to the apostles. 34 However, it seemed good to Silas to remain there. 35 Paul and Barnabas also remained in Antioch, teaching and preaching the word of the Lord, with many others also.

Paul and Barnabas with others made the long journey to Jerusalem. Their hearts must have been warmed by the reception they received on their travels. Again, a welcome awaited them in Jerusalem. It was very different from the one Paul received as a comparatively new convert a few years before. Then, Paul was greeted with fear and suspicion. It was his fellow missionary, Barnabas, who befriended him at that time, and introduced him to the apostles.

The council of Jerusalem provides us with an example for all subsequent churches and organisations to follow. All the parties of the dispute were present. Everyone was allowed to have their say, and then the acknowledged leader or "chair" gave a reasoned judgement which was accepted by all present.God's people do well to consult. So often there are those who wish to use the church as a tool for the gaining and the use of power. We should ask the question, "Is what I suggest agreeable to Scripture, and therefore does it conform to God's will?" The kingdom of God means that God rules, and therefore our advancement, our projection, our ambition is in total subjection to His will. We should never hesitate to take advice.

This is something that the Apostle Peter learnt the hard way. Jesus was patient with him and the tone of his contribution was evidence of that. Peter, the changed man, made some important points.

Firstly, the Gentiles received the Holy Spirit in the same way as they did. God made no distinction between Jew and Gentile.

Secondly, he could see that the usual interpretation of the Law was a burden that no-one could cope with. This is something that Pharisees and the equivalent modern legalists never seem to understand.

Thirdly, it was by grace, that is God's unmerited favour on undeserving sinners that we are saved. To summarize Peter, (v 11) "We are saved in the same manner as they." Peter, years later, wrote:

Whom having not seen you love. Though now you do not see Him, yet believing, you rejoice with joy inexpressible and full of glory, receiving the end of your faith the salvation of your souls. (1 Pet 1: 8-9)

Once learnt, it was a concept Peter never forgot.

The summary of James was from a man who was initially resistant to his half-brother, Jesus, (John 7: 5)but after the resurrection, James became a pillar and leader of the church in Jerusalem.

He listened to the evidence from everyone and quoted a relevant passage concerning the Gentiles. (Amos 9: 11-12)

He agreed with the mission to the Gentiles and did not insist on circumcision. To help the Pharisees present he suggested some reasonable rules. A sign of a converted heart is abstinence from sexual immorality. Sexual acts were all part of pagan temple practice. The convert would have to turn his or her back on that completely. Paul and Barnabas were in total agreement with that ruling.

The modern world is highly sexualised and the Christian has to make a decision to live a life of sexual purity against the tide of prevailing opinion.

It is encouraging to note that the letter to all the churches explaining the decisions referred to the apostles and elders as brothers. It was a term of fellowship and endearment, which is so often lacking from the pronouncements from many leading denominations. No matter who we are, and how senior we may be, the new convert is our sister or brother.

The term, "It seemed good to the Holy Spirit and to us," (v 28) is one that shows the importance of godly harmony. In other words, since the Holy Spirit had demonstrated His gift to the Gentiles then that settled the matter.

The judgement pronounced at that Jerusalem council so long ago paved the way for a worldwide church, for which we should all be profoundly grateful.

Acts 15:36-41

36 Then after some days Paul said to Barnabas, "Let us now go back and visit our brethren in every city where we have preached the word of the Lord, and see how they are doing." 37 Now Barnabas was determined to take with them John called Mark. 38 But Paul insisted that they should not take with them the one who had departed from them in Pamphylia, and had not gone with them to the work. 39 Then the contention became so sharp that they parted from one another. And so Barnabas took Mark and sailed to Cyprus; 40 but Paul chose Silas and departed, being commended by the brethren to the grace of God. 41 And he went through Syria and Cilicia, strengthening the churches.

This part of Acts described an incident that was challenging and, in a perverse way, encouraging. Many have argued against the veracity of scripture, but a piece of fiction would not have included this story and many other biblical stories, which have placed the main characters in a less than flattering light.

The two principal characters had worked and suffered together for the sake of the gospel. They had been friends for years. Barnabas, at the beginning of their partnership, had shown unusual support and loyalty towards Paul, when everyone else was mistrustful and fearful.

The question they faced, and it is a recurrent question, was: What was more important, the man, his potential and personal development, or the task in front of them? Barnabas wanted to give his relative, John Mark, a second chance, but Paul had felt profoundly let down by Mark's previous departure from the mission field.

Barnabas, a 'people person', saw great potential in Mark, and felt that they should risk his inclusion. Paul considered that Mark would endanger the next missionary journey, which would go further into the mainland of Asia. The disagreement was so intense; the Greek used here is the word from which we get the word, "paroxysms". Consequently, the two great servants of God parted company.

So who was right? In a sense both were right, but the argument could have been carried out far more peaceably.

Paul later wrote to the Corinthians:

Love suffers long and is kind; love does not envy; love does not parade itself, is not puffed up; does not behave rudely, does not seek its own, is not provoked, thinks no evil; does not rejoice in iniquity, but rejoices in the truth; bears all things, believes all things, hopes all things, endures all things. Love never fails. (1 Cor 13: 4-8)

Barnabas, "that son of encouragement", took Mark with him to Cyprus. It is marvellous to know that God gives us a second chance after we have let Him down. A similar thing had happened centuries before in the case of Jonah. After Jonah's flight from the will of God, "The word of the Lord came to Jonah a second time." (Jonah 3: 1) We all can and should take encouragement from that.

Mark later penned the wonderful Gospel that bears his name. Furthermore, he was restored to friendship with Paul, (2 Tim 4:11) and became a chief assistant to Peter, who looked on him as a son. (1 Pet 5: 13)

Paul took Silas with him. This was an advantage since Silas, unlike Barnabas, was also a Roman citizen. The outcome was to be for the best.

We are not told how Mark felt about the argument that was centred on him. It is probable that he was aware of it at the time and that it caused great distress and annoyance to him. As far as we can tell, Barnabas and indeed Paul, later, ensured that he did not suffer psychological damage or feelings of rejection. Other writers have not commented on this particular point.

If it is at all possible, and is within our power, we should try to get on with everyone. (Rom 12: 18) However, very rarely, we may have to part company, but this should be done only after much prayer. The last thing we should want to do is cause damage to the other person, the fellowship, the wider church, the cause of Christ, and His reputation.

At the beginning of each day, not only should we ask the question, what is my priority, but also, who is my priority?

Acts 16:1-10

1 Then he came to Derbe and Lystra. And behold, a certain disciple was there, named Timothy, the son of a certain Jewish woman who believed, but his father was Greek. 2 He was well spoken of by the brethren who were at Lystra and Iconium. 3 Paul wanted to have him go on with him. And he took him and circumcised him because of the Jews who were in that region, for they all knew that his father was Greek. 4 And as they went through the cities, they delivered to them the decrees to keep, which were determined by the apostles and elders at Jerusalem. 5 So the churches were strengthened in the faith, and increased in number daily. 6 Now when they had gone through Phrygia and the region of Galatia, they were forbidden by the Holy Spirit (or, "the Spirit of Jesus"), to preach the word in Asia. 7 After they had come to Mysia, they tried to go into Bithynia, but the Spirit did not permit them. 8 So passing by Mysia, they came down to Troas. 9 And a vision appeared to Paul in the night. A man of Macedonia stood and pleaded with him, saying, "Come over to Macedonia and help us." 10 Now after he had seen the vision, immediately we sought to go to Macedonia, concluding that the Lord had called us to preach the gospel to them.

The overland mission to Derbe, Lystra, the other places and churches, was one of consolidation, and distribution of the Jerusalem verdict. The Judaizing tendency was countered and the new converts were strengthened in their faith. Again, the church increased in numbers. Such growth is not seen today in Europe, but it is seen in other parts of the world. In China, in the last sixty years, the church has grown from around one million to tens of millions of Christians. This has happened in spite of continuing persecution, or perhaps because of it.

Previously, Paul had turned down a promising helper, John Mark. In Lystra, he found another, Timothy, to whom he became like a father. Paul, having made such an issue about the non-necessity of circumcision, circumcised Timothy. This was because his mother was a Jewish believer, although his father was Greek. It was done because of expediency, so that they could visit Jewish synagogues and not run into arguments about issues of identity. As has already been noted, Paul later summed up the position he took:

And to the Jews I became as a Jew, that I might win Jews; to those who are under the law, as under the law, that I might win those who are under the law; to those who are without law, as without law (not being without law toward God, but under law toward Christ), that I might win those who are without law; to the weak I became as weak, that I might win the weak. I have become all things to all men, that I might by all means save some. (1 Cor 9: 20-22)

What a wonderful God we have who is willing to come right alongside us to save us, transform us and take us on into His life and kingdom.

After the visit to Psidian Antioch, the intrepid party travelled 500 miles without being able to preach. We are not told why, except, and suffice to say, the Spirit of Jesus would not allow them. (v 6)

At this point, it is worth noting, that the words, "Spirit of Jesus", and in the previous chapter, "Holy Spirit" (v 28) indicate a Divine unity. Although Jehovah's Witnesses, Mormons, Unitarians and others refuse to see it, the doctrine of the Trinity runs throughout the whole of the New Testament and indeed throughout the whole of the Bible.

This lack of preaching and gospel ministry must have seemed very frustrating and perplexing to a person like Paul, but these experiences can lead to an unanticipated sphere of service. For our part, we need to be committed and willing. On God's part, He is a God of surprises. Where one door closes, another may open.

Then, at last, there was a breakthrough. The vision of the man from Macedonia provided a new area for action. It was a very significant development. Commentators have made much about this move into Europe. However, at that time, the move would not have been seen as so striking because, Macedonia, still bordered the Mediterranean, was still part of the Roman Empire, and the universal language was still Greek.

Acts 16:11-15

11 Therefore, sailing from Troas, we ran a straight course to Samothrace, and the next day came to Neapolis, **12** and from there to Philippi, which is the foremost city of that part of Macedonia, a colony. And we were staying in that city for some days. **13** And on the Sabbath day we went out of the city to the riverside, where prayer was customarily made; and we sat down and spoke to the women who met there. **14** Now a certain woman named Lydia heard us. She was a seller of purple from the city of Thyatira, who worshiped God. The Lord opened her heart to heed the things spoken by Paul. **15** And when she and her household were baptized, she begged us, saying, "If you have judged me to be faithful to the Lord, come to my house and stay." So she persuaded us.

Paul's vision was of a man, but the first person to become a Christian in Philippi was a woman. She is the fifth woman to be named in Acts. In many ways, Lydia would be regarded today as a role model for the modern liberated woman. She was intelligent, articulate, confident, and a woman of means. She dealt with and sold purple cloth to the upper classes. She lived in a substantial residence. Yet in other ways, she did not fit the secular picture of a modern woman.

In the first place, she feared God. The secure mercantile position that she enjoyed was not enough. The chances and changes of this uncertain world made her dissatisfied with a mere secular worldview. She believed and worshiped God.

In the second place, she was a woman of prayer. The God that she believed in was not a Greek-type deity, capricious and unreliable being, but a just, holy creator God who was concerned about the day-to-day activities of women and men.

In the third place, although there were a few like-minded women, with whom she would meet regularly for prayer, there were not enough Jews to form a synagogue. The custom to meet by a river possibly dated back to the Jewish Babylonian captivity. However, although she was a busy person, Lydia considered it important to meet with fellow believers for prayer. If any one had an excuse to be too busy, it was Lydia.

In the fourth place, she responded to Paul's message and gave her heart and life to Christ. She demonstrated the sign of a converted heart by showing a generous heart in the invitation to Paul and his friends to stay at her house.

Finally, she and her whole household were baptised. We need to remember that baptism was preceded by faith. There are many in this world who think that the act of baptism itself confers some religious input into a person and "Christianises" them. Baptism is a powerful symbol that signifies a number of things, including new life, and the washing away of sins. It is not magic. It is sobering to note that some of the world's great tyrants were baptized (as infants), but ultimately they were opponents of Christianity.

Before leaving this passage, it should be noted that the early Christians in Philippi were devout women who made an enormous contribution to the beginning of that church. J. C. Ryle, the Victorian bishop, and described as a man of granite with the heart of a child, made these remarks when commenting on Luke 8: 1-3:

It was not a woman who sold the Lord for thirty pieces of silver. They were not women who forsook the Lord in the garden and fled. It was not a woman who denied him three times in the high priest's house. —But they were women who lamented when Jesus was led forth to be crucified. They were women who stood to the last by the cross. And they were women who were first to visit the grave "where the Lord lay." Great indeed is the power of the grace of God. (J. C. Ryle, Expository Thoughts on the Gospels.)

It was a woman, Mary Magdelene, who was the first witness to the risen Lord. In subsequent history, women with men have died for their faith. We should all thank God for the faith and witness of women.

Acts 16:16-24

16 Now it happened, as we went to prayer, that a certain slave girl possessed with a spirit of divination met us, who brought her masters much profit by fortune-telling. **17** This girl followed Paul and us, and cried out, saying, "These men are the servants of the Most High God, who proclaim to us the way of salvation." **18** And this she did for many days. But Paul, greatly annoyed, turned and said to the spirit, "I command you in the name of Jesus Christ to come out of her." And he came out that very hour. **19** But when her masters saw that their hope of profit was gone, they seized Paul and Silas and dragged them into the marketplace to the authorities. **20** And they brought them to the magistrates, and said, "These men, being Jews, exceedingly trouble our city; **21** and they teach customs which are not lawful for us, being Romans, to receive or observe." **22** Then the multitude rose up together against them; and the magistrates tore off their clothes and commanded them to be beaten with rods. **23** And when they had laid many stripes on them, they threw them into prison, commanding the jailer to keep them securely. **24** Having received such a charge, he put them into the inner prison and fastened their feet in the stocks.

Human trafficking has been present since the beginning of history. People have been used and abused in many ways and this girl who was demonised, as a fortune-teller, was one such instance. It reminds us that the practice of crystal ball gazing, fortune telling, séances, tarot cards, and horoscopes are not mere fun but potentially very dangerous. No doubt this girl was trapped and had no escape. She was bought in the market place and could be sold in the market place. Many men will go to terrible lengths to gain cash. In spite of all the progress of recent decades, illegal human trafficking and modern slavery is a multi-billion dollar industry. It has a dreadful grip on countless lives.

In a number of New Testament passages, the demons knew who Jesus was. The demons knew that they would be judged. They knew that Jesus is more powerful than they. (Luke 4:34) In this instance, the slave girl knew that the missionary group were from God and that they preached the way of salvation. James also mentions this uncanny demonic awareness:

You believe that there is one God. You do well. Even the demons believe and tremble! (James 2:19)

We should note the deep concern, disquiet and patience of Paul and his friends. They had a number of options. They could ask the slave girl to go away. They could bribe her owners to remove her. Paul after much thought, exorcised her. With that, she lost the power to behave in her strange and disturbing ways, and lost the power to gain money for her owners. She was expendable and no doubt discarded. We are not told what happened to her, but the local believers would have provided or directed her to a safe house if she was able and willing to escape. The need for safe houses for abused women, prostitutes and trafficked people remains to this day and has become an increasingly important ministry.

Jesus taught that if one demon had been cast out then the void could be taken up by an even greater evil. How true this is. Not only do we see this in people but also in nations. The downfall of an evil tyrant or dictator can be followed by something worse, namely, a whole group of competing warlords.

How important it is that if evil or an evil spirit is removed from someone's life, the spiritual vacuum should be filled not by another set of demons, but the Holy Spirit. (Luke 11:24-26)

Up to that time, opposition to Christ and his followers was based on what might be called doctrine. Many Jews rejected Jesus as their Messiah, and these believers were regarded as threatening the status of the Jewish leadership. Later Jewish authorities described Jesus as the man who led many in Israel astray. In this passage, the issue is money.

So often Christians are left alone until the influence of the gospel hits the pocket of those who have a vested interest in godless and God-resisting pastimes. Then all kinds of other objections are brought to the surface. The objection in this passage was that Paul was allegedly teaching customs that were unlawful for Romans since Christianity was not a recognized religion. The irony was, that it was unlawful for the magistrates to order the flogging and punishment to Paul and Silas, because they were Roman citizens and were exempt from such treatment without a proper trial.

Acts 16:25-40

25 But at midnight Paul and Silas were praying and singing hymns to God, and the prisoners were listening to them. **26** Suddenly there was a great earthquake, so that the foundations of the prison were shaken; and immediately all the doors were opened and everyone's chains were loosed. **27** And the keeper of the prison, awaking from sleep and seeing the prison doors open, supposing the prisoners had fled, drew his sword and was about to kill himself. **28** But Paul called with a loud voice, saying, "Do yourself no harm, for we are all here." **29** Then he called for a light, ran in, and fell down trembling before Paul and Silas. **30** And he brought them out and said, "Sirs, what must I do to be saved?" **31** So they said, "Believe on the Lord Jesus Christ, and you will be saved, you and your household." **32** Then they spoke the word of the Lord to him and to all who were in his house. **33** And he took them the same hour of the night and washed their stripes. And immediately he and all his family were baptized. **34** Now when he had brought them into his house, he set food before them; and he rejoiced, having believed in God with all his household. **35** And when it was day, the magistrates sent the officers, saying, "Let those men go." **36** So the keeper of the prison reported these words to Paul, saying, "The magistrates have sent to let you go. Now therefore depart, and go in peace." **37** But Paul said to them, "They have beaten us openly, uncondemned Romans, and have thrown us into prison. And now do they put us out secretly? No indeed! Let them come themselves and get us out." **38** And the officers told these words to the magistrates, and they were afraid when they heard that they were Romans. **39** Then they came and pleaded with them and brought them out, and asked them to depart from the city. **40** So they went out of the prison and entered the house of Lydia; and when they had seen the brethren, they encouraged them and departed.

The story of the conversion of the Philippian jailer contains a number of note-worthy points.

The first point is the serenity and courage of Paul and Silas. They had been beaten so severely that blood was running off their backs. They were fastened so securely in the stocks that they had little room for movement. And yet, instead of feeling sorry and grumbling between themselves, they were praying and singing psalms; what a surprise, what a paradox. They trusted God to such an extent that, although they would not have known what was coming, they believed that God was in control and would keep them safe in eternity.

The second point relates to the earthquake. Although the building shook, the doors opened, and the chains fell off, no-one moved, no-one was injured, and all were quiet. The natural phenomenon of an earthquake was accompanied by supernatural consequences.

Thirdly, the jailer, who was probably a tough retired Roman Centurion, had become a quivering wreck. If he was found responsible for the escape of prisoners, then his own life was at risk. He thought he would pre-empt things by falling on his sword. Paul stopped him and reassured him all were still in place. The trembling man then fell at the feet of those he had treated so cruelly. He asked the most important question that can ever be asked, "What can I do to be saved?" But did he understand what he was saying? We can assume that he knew that Paul and Silas were religious teachers, and may have heard amidst the clamour that they preached a way of salvation. Paul and Silas had something that he did not. He understood sufficiently to be able to grasp onto the reply, "Believe in the Lord Jesus and you will be saved." (v 31) That night, he found faith in Christ, as did his household.

The fourth point is the change in the man's life and demeanour. The man who breathed hate and inflicted injuries became the man who washed and dressed the wounds of his former victims. As he did this, he heard more from Paul and Silas about the Jesus in whom he had come to believe. Not only had he received eternal salvation, but he had begun a journey of behaviour transformation. The man of hate had become the man of kindness. The man was of middle age. Rarely do those who are settled in their ways come naturally to faith in Christ. It usually takes a tremor, bereavement, or a tragedy to make them think again. Unlike Lydia and Cornelius who were God-fearers and ready to make a move towards Christ, it was the last thing on the jailer's mind when he had woken up that previous morning.

The fifth point is the coincidental "back-tracking" of the magistrates who overnight ordered the release of the two prisoners. They became alarmed when they learnt that Paul and Silas were Roman citizens, and that they had been punished without having had a trial. Paul's insistence that the magistrates should escort them out of prison in full view of the populace probably conferred a legal protection on the emerging church. There are times when we should insist on our rights, and times when we should not. We need to pray that we make the right decision. Insistence on our rights should usually be associated with the help it can give to others, as in this case.

The final point is the observation that both here and in general experience, the Christian church brings together people who would not normally meet, associate or socialize with one another. Lydia and the jailer were two entirely different people, and yet they had become members of the same fellowship. The church in Philippi had a special place in Paul's heart. In his later letter, he wrote towards the beginning:

I thank my God upon every remembrance of you, always in every prayer of mine making request for you all with joy, for your fellowship in the gospel from the first day until now, being confident of this very thing, that He who has begun a good work in you will complete it until the day of Jesus Christ. (Phil 1: 3-6)

The church of Philippi was a generous and giving church. Later, when Paul was in need, they alone sent aid. (Phil 4: 14-16) May God give us all generous hearts! (2 Cor 9: 7)

Acts 17:1-15

1 Now when they had passed through Amphipolis and Apollonia, they came to Thessalonica, where there was a synagogue of the Jews. 2 Then Paul, as his custom was, went in to them, and for three Sabbaths reasoned with them from the Scriptures, 3 explaining and demonstrating that the Christ had to suffer and rise again from the dead, and saying, "This Jesus whom I preach to you is the Christ." 4 And some of them were persuaded; and a great multitude of the devout Greeks, and not a few of the leading women, joined Paul and Silas. 5 But the Jews who were not persuaded, becoming envious, took some of the evil men from the marketplace, and gathering a mob, set all the city in an uproar and attacked the house of Jason, and sought to bring them out to the people. 6 But when they did not find them, they dragged Jason and some brethren to the rulers of the city, crying out, "These who have turned the world upside down have come here too. 7 Jason has harbored them, and these are all acting contrary to the decrees of Caesar, saying there is another king--Jesus." 8 And they troubled the crowd and the rulers of the city when they heard these things. 9 So when they had taken security from Jason and the rest, they let them go. 10 Then the brethren immediately sent Paul and Silas away by night to Berea. When they arrived, they went into the synagogue of the Jews. 11 These were more fair-minded than those in Thessalonica, in that they received the word with all readiness, and searched the Scriptures daily to find out whether these things were so. 12 Therefore many of them believed, and also not a few of the Greeks, prominent women as well as men. 13 But when the Jews from Thessalonica learned that the word of God was preached by Paul at Berea, they came there also and stirred up the crowds. 14 Then immediately the brethren sent Paul away, to go to the sea; but both Silas and Timothy remained there. 15 So those who conducted Paul brought him to Athens; and receiving a command for Silas and Timothy to come to him with all speed, they departed.

Paul and Silas had to leave Philippi but were undaunted in their task of proclaiming the gospel. On arrival in Thessalonica they pursued their normal practice of going to the synagogue. Here, Paul as usual in his ministry to the Jewish people gave an exposition from the Hebrew Scriptures. On reading the summary, we may be prompted to ask the questions: What sort of Messiah do you expect? What do we want the Messiah to be? What kind of Jesus should we follow? How do we picture our hero?

The Jews of that era expected a great ruler who would be set up in Jerusalem with an accompanying renewal of temple worship, which all nations would acknowledge. The idea that the Messiah would suffer and die on a cross and rise again was an offensive stumbling block. However, Paul with his complete knowledge of the Hebrew Scriptures took his hearers through each text line-by-line and demonstrated that the Messiah should do just that. One passage, which emphasises the sufferings of the Messiah, is Isaiah chapter fifty-three:

But He was wounded for our transgressions, He was bruised for our iniquities; The chastisement for our peace was upon Him, And by His stripes we are healed. (Isaiah 53: 5)

Just as with the Jews of old, there are many today, both inside and outside the churches who are appalled by the idea that the sufferings and crucifixion of Christ in any way bring salvation. One such author has recently described the cross as "cosmic child abuse".

We need to hold onto the fact that Jesus was a sacrifice for sin and that He took the punishment for our past, present and future sins on that cross. Hallelujah! What a Saviour!

Most of our heroes are good-looking, athletic and some are intelligent. Whilst Jesus had a supreme intelligence, he is described as a "man of sorrows and acquainted with grief". (Isaiah 53: 3)

Whilst Jesus may not be what most consider to look like a hero, He remains, author of creation, the light of the world, the way the truth and the life, and the only Saviour.

The response to Paul's ministry was striking. It saw the beginnings of a sizable church that included both Jews and Gentiles. However, the peaceful progress was short-lived. Luke states that the cause of opposition was religious jealousy. A dangerous form of jealousy can arise from inside the church, when one group appears to be more successful than another. May we guard ourselves against all kinds of jealousy.

The jealousy described here in Acts generated mob violence and Jason and other innocent people were seized. The atmosphere had become toxic, causing the rapid departure of Paul and Silas southwards to Berea.

Although the Bible describes the Bereans as more noble, after early success, once again the situation deteriorated, and Paul became a fugitive as he travelled towards Athens.

Acts 17:16-18

16 Now while Paul waited for them at Athens, his spirit was provoked within him when he saw that the city was given over to idols. **17** Therefore he reasoned in the synagogue with the Jews and with the Gentile worshipers, and in the marketplace daily with those who happened to be there. **18** Then certain Epicurean and Stoic philosophers encountered him. And some said, "What does this babbler want to say?" Others said, "He seems to be a proclaimer of foreign gods," because he preached to them Jesus and the resurrection.

Athens resembled modern European culture, perhaps more than any other place on Paul's journeys. In its heyday, the city was a centre for art, philosophy and literature. People gave the appearance of being all-sufficient.

In this passage, we see some aspects of Paul's character, which should be present in every Christian.

Firstly, he was deeply troubled to see a city full of idols. Although we do not see many idols around, Hindu and Buddhist idols are fashionable items that furnish some people's homes. Even though many have little interest in God and atheism is advancing, the culture is full of the idols of money, self, celebrity, sex, sport and food. If the idols of Athens troubled Paul, we should be troubled by today's idols.

Secondly, he had a compassionate heart, and visited the synagogue and the market place to speak about salvation through Christ. We should try to alleviate suffering. We should work for a good education for all. We should support measures that create jobs, but the most compassionate thing we can do for someone is to tell them about Christ.

Thirdly, he had spiritual stamina. Paul had been thrown out of various cities and his life was at risk. He was concerned about the wellbeing of the churches of Philippi, Thessalonica, and Berea and was anxious to receive news about them. He was awaiting his friends and was apprehensive about their safety. Moreover, he was tired from a long journey and had every reason to rest, and yet, he made it his priority share the gospel. So often we seek an excuse to say, pray or do nothing.

We should bring these qualities before God in prayer and ask Him to build us up day by day.

We are told in this passage about Paul's encounter with philosophy. Philosophy and Christianity have always had a problematic relationship. We should not despise philosophy, for the great thinkers and intellects of the world can have much to teach us. After all, the book of Ecclesiastes can be regarded as a treatise of philosophy. The problem is that so much of philosophy is centred on humanity, and the power of the human intellect alone. Philosophers, in the main, are unable to agree with the worldview that God, who is our loving creator and redeemer, has disclosed Himself through the written word and the revealed word. The philosopher has difficulty with the whole idea of revelation. Although Paul had a powerful intellect and knew much about Greek thought, he wrote this to the Corinthians:

For the message of the cross is foolishness to those who are perishing, but to us who are being saved it is the power of God. For it is written: "I will destroy the wisdom of the wise, And bring to nothing the understanding of the prudent." Where is the wise? Where is the scribe? Where is the disputer of this age? Has not God made foolish the wisdom of this world? (1 Cor 1: 18-20)

In Athens, Paul's witnessed the clash between the cynicism of the philosophers and the challenge of Christianity.

Acts 17:19-34

19 And they took him and brought him to the Areopagus, saying, "May we know what this new doctrine is of which you speak? **20** For you are bringing some strange things to our ears. Therefore we want to know what these things mean." **21** For all the Athenians and the foreigners who were there spent their time in nothing else but either to tell or to hear some new thing. **22** Then Paul stood in the midst of the Areopagus and said, "Men of Athens, I perceive that in all things you are very religious; **23** for as I was passing through and considering the objects of your worship, I even found an altar with this inscription: TO THE UNKNOWN GOD. Therefore, the One whom you worship without knowing, Him I proclaim to you: **24** God, who made the world and everything in it, since He is Lord of heaven and earth, does not dwell in temples made with hands. **25** Nor is He worshiped with men's hands, as though He needed anything, since He gives to all life, breath, and all things. **26** And He has made from one blood every nation of men to dwell on all the face of the earth, and has determined their preappointed times and the boundaries of their dwellings, **27** so that they should seek the Lord, in the hope that they might grope for Him and find Him, though He is not far from each one of us; **28** for in Him we live and move and have our being, as also some of your own poets have said, 'For we are also His offspring.' **29** Therefore, since we are the offspring of God, we ought not to think that the Divine Nature is like gold or silver or stone, something shaped by art and man's devising. **30** Truly, these times of ignorance God overlooked, but now commands all men everywhere to repent, **31** because He has appointed a day on which He will judge the world in righteousness by the Man whom He has ordained. He has given assurance of this to all by raising Him from the dead." **32** And when they heard of the resurrection of the dead, some mocked, while others said, "We will hear you again on this matter." **33** So Paul departed from among them. **34** However, some men joined him and believed, among them Dionysius the Areopagite, a woman named Damaris, and others with them.

Paul's speech to his hearers in Athens is one of the greatest sermons ever preached to a Gentile audience. It has been discussed, commented upon and the themes copied for centuries.

Firstly, Paul commented on what he saw and heard around him. Whilst there was a multiplicity of gods, there was a shrine to the unknown god. All bases were covered. They left nothing to chance.

However, some of his hearers, the Epicureans, held the view that creation just happened by chance. This is not unlike many modern thinkers. Paul emphasized that the world did not happen by chance but there is a supreme designer and creator. In other words, there is evidence of God's existence from design. God made the universe and He is the God of history. He placed humanity into peoples and nations.

Secondly, Paul quoted Greek writers, indicating his previous homework and ability to apply it. Christian witnesses should always be aware of the culture around them, and seek a bridge with the gospel.

Thirdly, there is a command by God to repent, and at this point Paul described the Lord Jesus as the one who is the just standard and instrument of judgement.

Fourthly, Paul asserts the validity of all this because of the overwhelming evidence for the resurrection of Jesus.

We need to ask ourselves. Do we believe in the God of creation? Do we believe in a future judgement? Do we believe in the resurrection of Jesus?

At this point, Paul was halted in his tracks. He was unable to go on and talk about God's love and salvation through faith in Him. His listeners had had their minds engaged but they wanted to move on. It seems that Paul's sermon had ended in failure. Compared with the response seen elsewhere in Acts, it appeared to be just that, but there were a handful or so of believers and today we would have been delighted and thought the enterprise a success.

The response in Athens is typical of today's Europe. No wonder the continent is in the doldrums, spiritually, economically and in other ways. Yet, we need to be thankful for what God is doing in the hearts and lives of His faithful people, people like Dionysius and Damaris who responded to the message and became believers. We will have varying degrees of success when we present the gospel, but we should never lose heart:

And let us not grow weary while doing good, for in due season we shall reap if we do not lose heart. (Gal 6: 9)

We need to understand that we may never know the effect we have on people. Sometimes the things we say for God are remembered only years later.

Acts 18:1-11

1 After these things Paul departed from Athens and went to Corinth. 2 And he found a certain Jew named Aquila, born in Pontus, who had recently come from Italy with his wife Priscilla (because Claudius had commanded all the Jews to depart from Rome); and he came to them. 3 So, because he was of the same trade, he stayed with them and worked; for by occupation they were tentmakers. 4 And he reasoned in the synagogue every Sabbath, and persuaded both Jews and Greeks. 5 When Silas and Timothy had come from Macedonia, Paul was compelled by the Spirit, and testified to the Jews that Jesus is the Christ. 6 But when they opposed him and blasphemed, he shook his garments and said to them, "Your blood be upon your own heads; I am clean. From now on I will go to the Gentiles." 7 And he departed from there and entered the house of a certain man named Justus, one who worshiped God, whose house was next door to the synagogue. 8 Then Crispus, the ruler of the synagogue, believed on the Lord with all his household. And many of the Corinthians, hearing, believed and were baptized. 9 Now the Lord spoke to Paul in the night by a vision, "Do not be afraid, but speak, and do not keep silent; 10 for I am with you, and no one will attack you to hurt you; for I have many people in this city." 11 And he continued there a year and six months, teaching the word of God among them.

When Paul arrived at Corinth, he was alone, short of money, without accommodation, anxious about the state of the churches he had planted, and anxious about the safety of his friends. He was, no doubt, again, tired from his missionary exertions, persecutions and long travel. Instead of a holiday he found friends and a change. Aquila and Priscilla were probably already believers and a delightful couple, who with other Jews, had been expelled from Rome. Like Paul, they were able to make a living from tent making.

So Paul joined the business, made some cash, and stayed in Priscilla and Aquila's house. No doubt, he paid for his board and lodging. As a keen worker with an engaging manner, the business would have prospered. On the Sabbath, because of his status as a Pharisee, he spoke in the synagogue. This allowed Paul to recuperate from his recent hectic past.

Paul testified that he was a man who lived by faith. (Gal 2: 20). However, that does not mean we should sit around meditating, and wait for things to happen. We need to commit the day to God and ask Him to lead us to the right people and make the right, honest decisions and work effectively. Paul did just that and so should we. Like his Master, Paul had a trade, and these accounts give a blessing upon hard work and earning a living. Whatever we do, it should all be done to God's glory. This occupation in the early days in Corinth was a good preparation for the founding of a great church. Great as it was, it had strengths and some desperate weaknesses, just like churches today.

The arrival of Silas and Timothy was great news for Paul. They were safe. The churches of the Macedonia were making good progress. The Philippian church had also provided finance so that Paul and his friends could now move into full-time ministry. Full-time Christian workers need to have a reasonable living but, like so many in today's world, they need to be able to adapt to the presenting circumstances. As pressure on the contemporary church grows, there will be fewer in full-time ministry.

Once again, the preaching of the gospel divided the synagogue and sadly, sometimes today it divides churches. Paul pre-empted expulsion from the synagogue by leaving it. He took half the congregation with him and set up a fellowship next door. Division is a move which often is messy, has unforeseen consequences and should never be undertaken lightly. When and if it happens, it should only be done when the gospel is at stake, as in this instance. Sadly it can be religious people who are the most stubborn in resistance to the gospel.

Paul at this point expected a further bout of violent persecution. Although Crispus, the synagogue ruler, had become a believer, there was sufficient opposition to cause trouble. At this point of fear and near crisis, God intervened.

The Lord spoke words of reassurance and encouragement in the form of a vision. From then on, the friends pressed on with their work in Corinth.

We may not have visions but if we pray, things happen. The story is told of a man in a crisis which involved hundreds of people. He went aside, knelt down in prayer, and brought the whole situation before God. When he arose from prayer, he knew exactly what to do, and the plan worked. In another instance, a man was informed by his doctor that he had a life-threatening condition that required chemotherapy. That evening, his mind in turmoil, he prayed. He then experienced a continuing feeling of envelopment by the love of God. Later, he slept soundly as a child.

A woman had spent a life on alcohol and drugs. She was a single mother and at the end of her tether. One day, in desperation, she prayed to the God she did not know. Then she experienced a vision of Jesus. The lady became a Christian, and later she began to attend church. Her life began on a path to recovery. We should not write off visions, but we should test them with Scripture and by results.

"Draw near to God and he will draw near you." (James 4: 8) We should always treasure those words and act upon them. Regular Bible reading and prayer stores up a great bank of spiritual investment, which comes out during times of illness, bereavement and many other trials.

Acts 18:12-17

12 When Gallio was proconsul of Achaia, the Jews with one accord rose up against Paul and brought him to the judgment seat, 13 saying, "This fellow persuades men to worship God contrary to the law." 14 And when Paul was about to open his mouth, Gallio said to the Jews, "If it were a matter of wrongdoing or wicked crimes, O Jews, there would be reason why I should bear with you. 15 But if it is a question of words and names and your own law, look to it yourselves; for I do not want to be a judge of such matters." 16 And he drove them from the judgment seat. 17 Then all the Greeks took Sosthenes, the ruler of the synagogue, and beat him before the judgment seat. But Gallio took no notice of these things.

In this passage a number of issues arise.

The first one is that after eighteen months of ministry in Corinth, Paul was seized and brought before a court. The fame and influence of the proconsul, Gallio, was known throughout the Roman Empire. If the decision went against Paul, then not only would Paul face a cruel punishment, but Christianity would be made illegal everywhere and would have to go underground, as it did years later when believers were more numerous.

Secondly, this must have tested Paul's faith. Anyone who lives by faith will be tested, but whatever the outcome, in the end, Jesus triumphs. Even the cross was a triumph.

And you, being dead in your trespasses and the uncircumcision of your flesh, He has made alive together with Him, having forgiven you all trespasses, having wiped out the handwriting of requirements that was against us, which was contrary to us. And He has taken it out of the way, having nailed it to the cross. Having disarmed principalities and powers, He made a public spectacle of them, triumphing over them in it. (Col 2:13-15)

As for Paul, he had an inner strength, which came from God. Later he wrote:

As it is written: "For Your sake we are killed all day long; We are accounted as sheep for the slaughter." Yet in all these things we are more than conquerors through Him who loved us. For I am persuaded that neither death nor life, nor angels nor principalities nor powers, nor things present nor things to come, nor height nor depth, nor any other created thing, shall be able to separate us from the love of God which is in Christ Jesus our Lord. (Rom 8: 36-39)

In the event, Gallio was wise enough not to enter into a religious dispute between Jews. He threw the case out and ignored the follow-up when the crowd turned their anger from Paul to Sosthenes, the synagogue ruler who appeared to have brought the case in the first instance. He was lashed by way of punishment.

Thirdly, poor Sosthenes was mentioned in the beginning of Paul's first letter to the Corinthians as a brother. At some point, Sosthenes gave his life to the Messiah he had once rejected. Even those most opposed to Christianity can change. It happened to Paul, It happened to Sosthenes, and it happens today. Paul later wrote to Timothy:

Although I was formerly a blasphemer, a persecutor, and an insolent man; but I obtained mercy because I did it ignorantly in unbelief. And the grace of our Lord was exceedingly abundant, with faith and love which are in Christ Jesus. This is a faithful saying and worthy of all acceptance, that Christ Jesus came into the world to save sinners, of whom I am chief. (1 Tim 1: 13- 15)

Ever since they were written, these words have encouraged believers in their journeys of faith.

Acts 18:18-28

18 So Paul still remained a good while. Then he took leave of the brethren and sailed for Syria, and Priscilla and Aquila were with him. He had his hair cut off at Cenchrea, for he had taken a vow. **19** And he came to Ephesus, and left them there; but he himself entered the synagogue and reasoned with the Jews. **20** When they asked him to stay a longer time with them, he did not consent, **21** but took leave of them, saying, "I must by all means keep this coming feast in Jerusalem; but I will return again to you, God willing." And he sailed from Ephesus. **22** And when he had landed at Caesarea, and gone up and greeted the church, he went down to Antioch. **23** After he had spent some time there, he departed and went over the region of Galatia and Phrygia in order, strengthening all the disciples. **24** Now a certain Jew named Apollos, born at Alexandria, an eloquent man and mighty in the Scriptures, came to Ephesus. **25** This man had been instructed in the way of the Lord; and being fervent in spirit, he spoke and taught accurately the things of the Lord, though he knew only the baptism of John. **26** So he began to speak boldly in the synagogue. When Aquila and Priscilla heard him, they took him aside and explained to him the way of God more accurately. **27** And when he desired to cross to Achaia, the brethren wrote, exhorting the disciples to receive him; and when he arrived, he greatly helped those who had believed through grace; **28** for he vigorously refuted the Jews publicly, showing from the Scriptures that Jesus is the Christ.

Since they accompanied Paul on his journey to Ephesus, it is worth saying something about Priscilla and Aquila.

In Acts we are introduced to numerous believers. Many of them were fine Christians, who are for us examples of Godly living. This chapter refers repeatedly to this married couple. It was not easy to take Paul into their household. I am sure that he was good company and made a significant contribution to their lives, but his presence and witness to the gospel eventually brought a whole new group into the fellowship and wrought havoc with some of the locals, and clashes with the authorities. The growing church was no longer a group of like-minded, ordered individuals but attracted those from all walks of life, and even from the most scandalous.

Paul later wrote:

Do you not know that the unrighteous will not inherit the kingdom of God? Do not be deceived. Neither fornicators, nor idolaters, nor adulterers, nor homosexuals, nor sodomites, nor thieves, nor covetous, nor drunkards, nor revilers, nor extortioners will inherit the kingdom of God. And such were some of you. But you were washed, but you were sanctified, but you were justified in the name of the Lord Jesus and by the Spirit of our God. (1 Cor 6: 9-11)

This influx of people, tramping through the house, would have put strains on many marriages. However Priscilla and Aquila, not only put up with it they seem to have thrived on it. As a Christian married couple, they displayed certain great qualities.

Firstly, they were committed to Christ and the gospel. It would have been so easy to say that they were busy and given the minimum required, half-hearted service, as so many do. It is important for Christians to apportion their time wisely between Church, family, work, friends and each other. The important thing is that God is at the centre of all of it. " And a threefold cord is not quickly broken." (Ecc 4: 12)

Secondly, they were committed to the church. Not only did they adapt to the drama of a growing church, they gave instructional help to an up and coming speaker and debater, namely Apollos. They did not gossip to others over lunch about any doctrinal fault Apollos had, but brought him quietly into the hospitality of their home to help him advance in his understanding and witness.

Thirdly, they were committed to Paul in spite of all the controversy that surrounded his ministry. When Paul left to sail to Syria, they sold up the business and their home in Corinth, and accompanied him to Ephesus. They clearly had a warm affection for the apostle and we are told that they even risked their lives for him. (Rom 16: 4)

Finally, they were committed to each other. They are always together when mentioned in the New Testament. They are an example of Christian marriage. Christian marriage is a great witness to the world and the Bible states that it is a demonstration of the love which Christ has for His church. (Eph 5: 22-33) We should do all we can to nurture Christian marriage.

Before we leave this passage, it is worth noting the vast distances Paul travelled. He probably took a gift to the believers in Jerusalem, and then undaunted, travelled by land, probably mainly on foot from Syrian Antioch through all the churches in the region of modern Turkey until he eventually arrived in Ephesus. By this time Paul was nearing fifty years of age, and most might have settled in some quiet ministry in a large city. But Paul never lost sight of his commission:

So that from Jerusalem and round about to Illyricum I have fully preached the gospel of Christ. And so I have made it my aim to preach the gospel, not where Christ was named, lest I should build on another man's foundation. (Rom 15: 19-20)

Acts 19:1-12

1 And it happened, while Apollos was at Corinth, that Paul, having passed through the upper regions, came to Ephesus. And finding some disciples 2 he said to them, "Did you receive the Holy Spirit when you believed?" So they said to him, "We have not so much as heard whether there is a Holy Spirit." 3 And he said to them, "Into what then were you baptized?" So they said, "Into John's baptism." 4 Then Paul said, "John indeed baptized with a baptism of repentance, saying to the people that they should believe on Him who would come after him, that is, on Christ Jesus." 5 When they heard this, they were baptized in the name of the Lord Jesus. 6 And when Paul had laid hands on them, the Holy Spirit came upon them, and they spoke with tongues and prophesied. 7 Now the men were about twelve in all. 8 And he went into the synagogue and spoke boldly for three months, reasoning and persuading concerning the things of the kingdom of God. 9 But when some were hardened and did not believe, but spoke evil of the Way before the multitude, he departed from them and withdrew the disciples, reasoning daily in the school of Tyrannus. 10 And this continued for two years, so that all who dwelt in Asia heard the word of the Lord Jesus, both Jews and Greeks. 11 Now God worked unusual miracles by the hands of Paul, 12 so that even handkerchiefs or aprons were brought from his body to the sick, and the diseases left them and the evil spirits went out of them.

When Paul arrived for the second time in Ephesus, he was on his third missionary journey. He worked in the region for up to three years. It is worth stating that during this time he was probably persecuted at the hands of the local Jewish population, and may have even spent some time in prison.

For we do not want you to be ignorant, brethren, of our trouble which came to us in Asia: that we were burdened beyond measure, above strength, so that we despaired even of life. Yes, we had the sentence of death in ourselves, that we should not trust in ourselves but in God who raises the dead, who delivered us from so great a death, and does deliver us; in whom we trust that He will still deliver us. (2 Cor 1: 8- 10)

Paul in his letter may have been talking about the riot in Ephesus alone, but it is sufficient to say that for good reasons the Holy Spirit does not include other persecutions in the narrative of Acts, although there is an implication in verse 9.The meeting with the disciples who were not yet true Christians is in a sense unique to that time. They were aware of the teaching of John the Baptist, and may have even understood that Jesus was their Messiah, but they probably knew very little about the cross and resurrection and nothing about the Holy Spirit and the day of Pentecost. These disciples were then baptized in the name of the Lord Jesus, and spoke in tongues after the "laying on of hands" Although not all Christians in those times spoke in tongues, the indwelling Christ by the Holy Spirit remains for all time a vital part of Christian experience.

For by one Spirit we were all baptized into one body whether Jews or Greeks, whether slaves or free and have all been made to drink into one Spirit. (1 Cor 12: 13)

Perhaps the nearest parallel today is the fact that there are thousands in or around the edges of our church buildings. They may have some sympathy, attend some services and events, and even give to the churches, but do not wish through the Holy Spirit to ask Christ into their lives. They clearly have some knowledge, but sadly, do not have saving faith. We need a deep burden to pray that more and more of these people come to true faith in the Lord Jesus.

It is remarkable that through the teaching and discussions in the "School of Tyrannus", and the missionary travels around the area, that all the residents of the province of Asia, " heard the word of the Lord Jesus". (v 10)

It is a fact that in the West today, more and more people know less and less about the Bible and the gospel; such is the power of secularism and unbelief. Let us remain faithful to the task of sharing, gossiping and proclaiming the gospel.

Extraordinary signs and wonders accompanied the ministry of Paul. We should be careful and be aware that the sweatbands and aprons were not lucky charms and had no powers themselves, but

God alone did the healings. Great harm has been done by the use of relics. There have been many superstitions that have persisted and have caused distortion to the true faith.

Acts 19:13-41

13 Then some of the itinerant Jewish exorcists took it upon themselves to call the name of the Lord Jesus over those who had evil spirits, saying, "We exorcise you by the Jesus whom Paul preaches." **14** Also there were seven sons of Sceva, a Jewish chief priest, who did so. **15** And the evil spirit answered and said, "Jesus I know, and Paul I know; but who are you?" **16** Then the man in whom the evil spirit was leaped on them, overpowered them, and prevailed against them, so that they fled out of that house naked and wounded. **17** This became known both to all Jews and Greeks dwelling in Ephesus; and fear fell on them all, and the name of the Lord Jesus was magnified. **18** And many who had believed came confessing and telling their deeds. **19** Also, many of those who had practiced magic brought their books together and burned them in the sight of all. And they counted up the value of them, and it totaled fifty thousand pieces of silver. **20** So the word of the Lord grew mightily and prevailed. **21** When these things were accomplished, Paul purposed in the Spirit, when he had passed through Macedonia and Achaia, to go to Jerusalem, saying, "After I have been there, I must also see Rome." **22** So he sent into Macedonia two of those who ministered to him, Timothy and Erastus, but he himself stayed in Asia for a time. **23** And about that time there arose a great commotion about the Way. **24** For a certain man named Demetrius, a silversmith, who made silver shrines of Diana, brought no small profit to the craftsmen. **25** He called them together with the workers of similar occupation, and said: "Men, you know that we have our prosperity by this trade. **26** Moreover you see and hear that not only at Ephesus, but throughout almost all Asia, this Paul has persuaded and turned away many people, saying that they are not gods which are made with hands. **27** So not only is this trade of ours in danger of falling into disrepute, but also the temple of the great goddess Diana may be despised and her magnificence destroyed, whom all Asia and the world worship." **28** Now when they heard this, they were full of wrath and cried out, saying, "Great is Diana of the Ephesians!" **29** So the whole city was filled with confusion, and rushed into the theater with one accord, having seized Gaius and Aristarchus, Macedonians, Paul's travel companions. **30** And when Paul wanted to go in to the people, the disciples would not allow him. **31** Then some of the officials of Asia, who were his friends, sent to him pleading that he would not venture into the theater. **32** Some therefore cried one thing and some another, for the assembly was confused, and most of them did not know why they had come together. **33** And they drew Alexander out of the multitude, the Jews putting him forward. And Alexander motioned with his hand, and wanted to make his defense to the people. **34** But when they found out that he was a Jew, all with one voice cried out for about two hours, "Great is Diana of the Ephesians!" **35** And when the city clerk had quieted the crowd, he said: "Men of Ephesus, what man is there who does not know that the city of the Ephesians is temple guardian of the great goddess Diana, and of the image which fell down from Zeus? **36** Therefore, since these things cannot be denied, you ought to be quiet and do nothing rashly. **37** For you have brought these men here who are neither robbers of temples nor blasphemers of your goddess. **38** Therefore, if Demetrius and his fellow craftsmen have a case against anyone, the courts are open and there are proconsuls. Let them bring charges against one another. **39** But if you have any other inquiry to make, it shall be determined in the lawful assembly. **40** For we are in danger of being called in question for today's uproar, there being no reason which we may give to account for this disorderly gathering." **41** And when he had said these things, he dismissed the assembly.

The strange episode concerning Jewish exorcists shows how true religion can be distorted. There are no direct instructions in the Torah (Old Testament Law) about exorcism and yet even a priest and his sons were employing devices and incantations on many needy people with varying success. Furthermore, it appeared that the accumulation of money and wealth was a key driving force in the development of their practice.

The most dangerous part of the process was that they clearly dabbled in the occult. Although they were not believers in Christ their Messiah, they saw the progress and success of the gospel in their town. So they used a new incantation, which involved the name of Jesus.

Then there was a demonstration of the danger of the occult when they tried to exorcize a certain individual. Although the demon knew Jesus and knew about Paul, he did not know the sons of Sceva and the man immediately attacked and overpowered them.

Paul had no doubt about the power of evil:

For we do not wrestle against flesh and blood, but against principalities, against powers, against the rulers of the darkness of this age, against spiritual hosts of wickedness in the heavenly places. (Eph 6: 12)

This story emphasizes the power of the occult. Jesus cannot be manipulated for any reason be it for exorcism, or the gain of influence and popularity, which some do in places where the church is strong. The point is that we should commit our lives to Him and ask Him to be our Lord. We cannot use, influence or manoeuvre God for our own selfish ends. God is a loving Father who knows what is best for us. Where there is true faith, there is the opportunity to resist the devil. (James 4: 7)

Paradoxically, this incident brought conviction to many who turned truly to Christ and became believers. The size of the response also affected the community in two ways. Firstly, there was a massive abandonment of witchcraft to the extent there was an enormous bonfire of extensive occult literature to the value of fifty thousand drachmas. Although comparisons are difficult this could be about five million pounds sterling or seven million U.S. dollars in today's money. The enlargement of the gospel brings cleansing to society.

After this, Paul felt he had an obligation to return to Jerusalem. He knew that the poor of Judea needed funds so he set up a collection in the surrounding churches and Macedonia so that he could take a gift with him.

Secondly, another economic wind was blowing. It is interesting that Paul did not preach specifically against the temple of Dianna and its accompanying pagan hideous worship. It is a lesson that we should be known primarily what we are for, rather than what we are against. Nevertheless, Paul would have stated that the gods built by human hands were not gods at all. The implication was there for all to see.

There was loss of trade by the Diana souvenir industry. Their protest sparked a riot. It is a terrifying thing to be the hate object of a riot. Gaius and Aristarchus, two doughty warriors of Christ were nearly lynched. Here we have an example of the loyalty and love of Paul towards his friends. He was prepared to intervene and stand up in front of the yelling mob and address them. In the event, his friends prevented him and the city clerk managed to calm things down and dismiss the crowd.

Are we committed to the Lord? Are we committed to other Christians in the way that Paul evidently was? We can never stop growing in grace and courage, if we wish.

Acts 20:1-16

1 After the uproar had ceased, Paul called the disciples to himself, embraced them, and departed to go to Macedonia. 2 Now when he had gone over that region and encouraged them with many words, he came to Greece 3 and stayed three months. And when the Jews plotted against him as he was about to sail to Syria, he decided to return through Macedonia. 4 And Sopater of Berea accompanied him to Asia--also Aristarchus and Secundus of the Thessalonians, and Gaius of Derbe, and Timothy, and Tychicus and Trophimus of Asia. 5 These men, going ahead, waited for us at Troas. 6 But we sailed away from Philippi after the Days of Unleavened Bread, and in five days joined them at Troas, where we stayed seven days. 7 Now on the first day of the week, when the disciples came together to break bread, Paul, ready to depart the next day, spoke to them and continued his message until midnight. 8 There were many lamps in the upper room where they were gathered together. 9 And in a window sat a certain young man named Eutychus, who was sinking into a deep sleep. He was overcome by sleep; and as Paul continued speaking, he fell down from the third story and was taken up dead. 10 But Paul went down, fell on him, and embracing him said, "Do not trouble yourselves, for his life is in him." 11 Now when he had come up, had broken bread and eaten, and talked a long while, even till daybreak, he departed. 12 And they brought the young man in alive, and they were not a little comforted. 13 Then we went ahead to the ship and sailed to Assos, there intending to take Paul on board; for so he had given orders, intending himself to go on foot. 14 And when he met us at Assos, we took him on board and came to Mitylene. 15 We sailed from there, and the next day came opposite Chios. The following day we arrived at Samos and stayed at Trogyllium. The next day we came to Miletus. 16 For Paul had decided to sail past Ephesus, so that he would not have to spend time in Asia; for he was hurrying to be at Jerusalem, if possible, on the Day of Pentecost.

Paul's decision to go to Jerusalem was associated with the desire to collect funds. It meant that he visited the young churches, and also gathered travelling companions with him. It would have been a great adventure for these young men. At each church, he would have made sure that teaching was a high priority.

The brief stay at Troas was a typical example. There are some valuable lessons to be learnt from it.

Firstly, they met together to break bread. Regular attendance at the Lord's Supper is important, because it is a memorial of the Lord's death on the cross. We so often easily forget what Jesus has done for us and this helps us remember that Jesus died in our place as a sacrifice for our sin, past, present and future.

As we partake of the bread and wine we feed on Christ by faith and we remember that one day He will come again.

In the first century, people sometimes absented themselves from these worship gatherings as they do today. The writer to the Hebrews urged his readers over this matter:

Not forsaking the assembling of ourselves together, as is the manner of some, but exhorting one another, and so much the more as you see the Day approaching (Heb 10: 25)

Secondly, they were all eager to be there and even stay listening to Paul all through the night. Today, some start to be restless even after five minutes! We need to be regular and expectant when we attend Christian worship because God may have a special word for us that day and we do not want to miss it.

Thirdly, like today, even the faithful nod off during prayers and the evening Sunday sermon. Poor Eutychus fell asleep and out of the window. He would have fallen three or four metres and may well have fractured his ribs and skull. Some of the fellowship thought he was dead. The actions of Paul are somewhat similar to those of Elijah. (1 Kings 17: 21) The process may have been miraculous and Luke does not say one way or another. In any case, his family were delighted, relieved and much comforted by his survival.

Falling asleep during a sermon is not to be commended. However, it is always better to become somnolent in the company of the Lord's people, rather than remaining at home on the excuse of tiredness and falling asleep in front of the television!In this passage we have an example of Paul's commitment to his people and his extraordinary stamina. He left that morning to resume his travels. We may become tired in the Lord's work. May we never become tired of the Lord's work. As Paul travelled he became increasingly aware of the danger of going to Jerusalem. Wherever he went, after a time, short or long, he suffered persecution. He knew that when he arrived in the centre of Jewish worship his presence there would arouse greater anger and conflict. Just as his Master set His face to go to Jerusalem, (Isaiah 50:7 and Luke 9: 51) so Paul committed himself to God and continued his journey.

The description of Paul's hurried journey along the coast of Asia Minor will be of great interest to those who love maps. It gives that sense of authenticity to the narrative.

Acts 20:17-38

17 From Miletus he sent to Ephesus and called for the elders of the church. **18** And when they had come to him, he said to them: "You know, from the first day that I came to Asia, in what manner I always lived among you, **19** serving the Lord with all humility, with many tears and trials which happened to me by the plotting of the Jews; **20** how I kept back nothing that was helpful, but proclaimed it to you, and taught you publicly and from house to house, **21** testifying to Jews, and also to Greeks, repentance toward God and faith toward our Lord Jesus Christ. **22** And see, now I go bound in the spirit to Jerusalem, not knowing the things that will happen to me there, **23** except that the Holy Spirit testifies in every city, saying that chains and tribulations await me. **24** But none of these things move me; nor do I count my life dear to myself, so that I may finish my race with joy, and the ministry which I received from the Lord Jesus, to testify to the gospel of the grace of God. **25** And indeed, now I know that you all, among whom I have gone preaching the kingdom of God, will see my face no more. **26** Therefore I testify to you this day that I am innocent of the blood of all men. **27** For I have not shunned to declare to you the whole counsel of God. **28** Therefore take heed to yourselves and to all the flock, among which the Holy Spirit has made you overseers, to shepherd the church of God which He purchased with His own blood. **29** For I know this, that after my departure savage wolves will come in among you, not sparing the flock. **30** Also from among yourselves men will rise up, speaking perverse things, to draw away the disciples after themselves. **31** Therefore watch, and remember that for three years I did not cease to warn everyone night and day with tears. **32** So now, brethren, I commend you to God and to the word of His grace, which is able to build you up and give you an inheritance among all those who are sanctified. **33** I have coveted no one's silver or gold or apparel. **34** Yes, you yourselves know that these hands have provided for my necessities, and for those who were with me. **35** I have shown you in every way, by laboring like this, that you must support the weak. And remember the words of the Lord Jesus, that He said, 'It is more blessed to give than to receive.' " **36** And when he had said these things, he knelt down and prayed with them all. **37** Then they all wept freely, and fell on Paul's neck and kissed him, **38** sorrowing most of all for the words which he spoke, that they would see his face no more. And they accompanied him to the ship

The farewell to the Ephesian elders is the only sermon or discourse in Acts given to Christian leaders. Paul began with a testimony about himself. Normally it is good practice not to talk about oneself when preaching or teaching. We all have a tendency to boast. Another good piece of advice is that if a personal story is told then the speaker should not be the hero.

Paul was accused of many things, but he was never accused of self-pride. His overriding concerns were the glory of God, the cause of the gospel, and the spiritual welfare of the people. To these ends, he was totally involved, physically, mentally, emotionally and spiritually. (v 19)

He was no overbearing, power obsessed boss. He was approachable, and dedicated, no matter the risk to himself. If we display only a part of that example, then we are on the right track.

Paul then emphasized in a few words the basics of becoming a Christian. They should continually ring in our ears and be declared by our lips, "Turn toward God in repentance and faith toward our Lord Jesus Christ." (v 21)

Paul talked about the value of his life. Elsewhere he made this comment:

For to me, to live is Christ, and to die is gain. But if I live on in the flesh, this will mean fruit from my labour; yet what I shall choose I cannot tell. For I am hard pressed between the two, having a desire to depart and be with Christ, which is far better. Nevertheless to remain in the flesh is more needful for you. (Phil 1: 21- 24)

For Paul, death did not have the terrors that it has for most people. (v 24) Like every Christian, however, he had the confidence and certainty of being safe with Christ after death. The Roman church, with its doctrine of purgatory, teaches that it is presumptuous to say that we can know that we are saved. Not only that, anyone who teaches assurance of salvation is pronounced accursed. However, thankfully, we do not depend on our own efforts but on the grace and promises of God, Indeed, since it is Biblical, we can and should have the assurance of salvation.

Nevertheless, death is the last enemy. Few of us go to bed one night, fit and well, and then die peacefully in our sleep. The process is frequently long, distressing, uncomfortable and sometimes painful. We are all aware from our own experience or that of others that we are outwardly decaying. The most important question is, "is the inward man being renewed day by day." (2 Cor 4:16)

It was said about the death of a young servant of Christ that he died 'full of Christian loveliness'. May that be said of all of us.

Paul went on to remind the elders of their great responsibility as guardians of the flock or people of God. God's people are of great value to God. They are a people bought with the great price of the blood of the Son of God. The price or penalty of our sin has been paid for by Jesus' death on the cross. (v 28)

The dangers that churches face are many. One of the gravest is false teachers, who are given the title of wolves, which savage the flock. It is a sad comment that the title included some of his listeners. Men seem to be so frequently ready to distort the gospel around their own particular likes, dislikes and pet theories.

May God grant that we stick closely to His Word.

Paul knew that churches could so easily go off track. Decades later, Jesus, in the book of Revelation, made this comment to the Ephesian church:

Nevertheless I have this against you, that you have left your first love. Remember therefore from where you have fallen; repent and do the first works, or else I will come to you quickly and remove your lampstand from its place unless you repent. (Rev 2: 4-5)

One of the first faults in that church was a tendency to embrace a nominal Christianity, which just goes through the motions and keeps faith to a minimum. This type of Christianity still occupies the chairs and pews of many of our churches.

It is a sobering thought that the most ravening wolf to fall on the churches in that part of the world came centuries later. Islam swept through and completely wiped out the Christian church except for a few small pockets. All that remained were the gospel truths that were planted in the first century and spread to the West and eventually to the rest of the world. Thankfully, we still have the epistles to those young churches. They still guide and still remain the word of life.

Paul, then as now, had his critics and was subject to accusations. Nearly all of it was and is totally unjustified. Many have, with varying success, tried to work out the psyche of this remarkable apostle. Whatever we might think, Paul's character endeared him to thousands of people. When some people leave an organization for the last time, often there is a sigh of relief. In Paul's case many tears were shed at the thought that they would never see him again. Christians should not be buttoned up. There is a right place for emotion.

Acts 21:1-26

1 Now it came to pass, that when we had departed from them and set sail, running a straight course we came to Cos, the following day to Rhodes, and from there to Patara. **2** And finding a ship sailing over to Phoenicia, we went aboard and set sail. **3** When we had sighted Cyprus, we passed it on the left, sailed to Syria, and landed at Tyre; for there the ship was to unload her cargo. **4** And finding disciples, we stayed there seven days. They told Paul through the Spirit not to go up to Jerusalem. **5** When we had come to the end of those days, we departed and went on our way; and they all accompanied us, with wives and children, till we were out of the city. And we knelt down on the shore and prayed. **6** When we had taken our leave of one another, we boarded the ship, and they returned home. **7** And when we had finished our voyage from Tyre, we came to Ptolemais, greeted the brethren, and stayed with them one day. **8** On the next day we who were Paul's companions departed and came to Caesarea, and entered the house of Philip the evangelist, who was one of the seven, and stayed with him. **9** Now this man had four virgin daughters who prophesied. **10** And as we stayed many days, a certain prophet named Agabus came down from Judea. **11** When he had come to us, he took Paul's belt, bound his own hands and feet, and said, "Thus says the Holy Spirit, 'So shall the Jews at Jerusalem bind the man who owns this belt, and deliver him into the hands of the Gentiles.' " **12** Now when we heard these things, both we and those from that place pleaded with him not to go up to Jerusalem. **13** Then Paul answered, "What do you mean by weeping and breaking my heart? For I am ready not only to be bound, but also to die at Jerusalem for the name of the Lord Jesus." **14** So when he would not be persuaded, we ceased, saying, "The will of the Lord be done." **15** And after those days we packed and went up to Jerusalem. **16** Also some of the disciples from Caesarea went with us and brought with them a certain Mnason of Cyprus, an early disciple, with whom we were to lodge. **17** And when we had come to Jerusalem, the brethren received us gladly. **18** On the following day Paul went in with us to James, and all the elders were present. **19** When he had greeted them, he told in detail those things which God had done among the Gentiles through his ministry. **20** And when they heard it, they glorified the Lord. And they said to him, "You see, brother, how many myriads of Jews there are who have believed, and they are all zealous for the law; **21** but they have been informed about you that you teach all the Jews who are among the Gentiles to forsake Moses, saying that they ought not to circumcise their children nor to walk according to the customs. **22** What then? The assembly must certainly meet, for they will hear that you have come. **23** Therefore do what we tell you: We have four men who have taken a vow. **24** Take them and be purified with them, and pay their expenses so that they may shave their heads, and that all may know that those things of which they were informed concerning you are nothing, but that you yourself also walk orderly and keep the law. **25** But concerning the Gentiles who believe, we have written and decided that they should observe no such thing, except that they should keep themselves from things offered to idols, from blood, from things strangled, and from sexual immorality." **26** Then Paul took the men, and the next day, having been purified with them, entered the temple to announce the expiration of the days of purification, at which time an offering should be made for each one of them.

Paul's journey to Jerusalem was by sea as far as Tyre and then by land. We can appreciate the concern they all had for Paul's safety. The intriguing account once again introduces us to some prophets. There are few instances of this type of prophecy today. What we do notice is the faithfulness of Agabus and the respect given Philip's four daughters who had a prophetic ministry. Agabus and others all warned Paul through the Holy Spirit of future danger. These spiritual insights did not deter Paul from his mission to go to Jerusalem. There are few of us who are prepared to face danger in the cause of the gospel.

Paul received a warm welcome on his arrival in Jerusalem. In association with his friends from the churches in far-off lands, he presented the gift, which had so diligently been brought together. Notice that Paul stated what God had done rather than boast about his own efforts. However, there was tension in the air. There were thousands of Jewish believers in The Way who still loved their traditional customs, temple worship and ceremonies. They still hankered after a kingdom restoration to Israel. They had erroneously believed rumours that Paul had encouraged the Jews in the European and other cities to depart from their traditions and customs, including circumcision. As far as we know Paul did not urge Jews against the practice of circumcision but he did make the important point that:

Circumcision is nothing and uncircumcision is nothing, but keeping the commandments of God is what matters. Let each one remain in the same calling in which he was called. (1 Cor 7: 19-20)

The account of the meeting between James and Paul teaches us the following:

Firstly, it is, in a sense, a model of disagreement or conflict resolution. James and Paul go out of their way to be courteous and gracious to one another. The elders rejoiced and praised God for the church growth amongst the Gentiles. They all agreed on the basics of the Faith, and James commended Paul for his integrity. Nevertheless, it was suggested that there had to be a gesture to the legalists, and a reassurance to them that Paul was still a practising Jew. A plan was put forward and Paul, at inconvenience to himself and no small financial cost, agreed. It is a fact of church life that there is often disagreement. It is crucial that the basics are maintained, but in other areas it is sometimes necessary to compromise. We need great discernment in this area. We all need gracious hearts, and it is more the pity they are not demonstrated more frequently.

Secondly, although James was surrounded by those who were zealous for the customs and temple ceremonies of Judaism, he makes no mention of these practices in his epistle. Jesus knows, and James knew the outworking of true religion:

Pure and undefiled religion before God and the Father is this: to visit orphans and widows in their trouble, and to keep oneself unspotted from the world. (James 1: 27)

Thirdly, there is one striking aspect to this part of the story. Up till then, in all the cities the Holy Spirit had warned the prophets and many believers about the dangers Paul was to face in Jerusalem. In a way, the danger was obvious, and Paul knew that he was actually going to fall into the hands of the Gentiles and be bound as a prisoner.

Unfortunately, the elders of the Jerusalem church seemed to be almost completely unaware of the dangers that Paul faced. Unlike the prophets of Caesarea, they were not so spiritually perceptive. Their joy and praise on hearing the news about all that God had done was Spirit-filled, but they seemed to lack the spiritual gift of understanding the future.

We all need to be able to discern the rightness of future plans.

Furthermore, we need to have an awareness and sensitivity to appreciate the dangers that our friends may have to face. We should not be gossips or busybodies but we need to be spiritually discerning when friends are in difficulty, for example, at work, or face strains in relationships, or are at risk of domestic violence. These are times when confidential help and prayer can be vital.

Acts 21:27-22:23

27 Now when the seven days were almost ended, the Jews from Asia, seeing him in the temple, stirred up the whole crowd and laid hands on him, **28** crying out, "Men of Israel, help! This is the man who teaches all men everywhere against the people, the law, and this place; and furthermore he also brought Greeks into the temple and has defiled this holy place." **29** (For they had previously seen Trophimus the Ephesian with him in the city, whom they supposed that Paul had brought into the temple.) **30** And all the city was disturbed; and the people ran together, seized Paul, and dragged him out of the temple; and immediately the doors were shut. **31** Now as they were seeking to kill him, news came to the commander of the garrison that all Jerusalem was in an uproar. **32** He immediately took soldiers and centurions, and ran down to them. And when they saw the commander and the soldiers, they stopped beating Paul. **33** Then the commander came near and took him, and commanded him to be bound with two chains; and he asked who he was and what he had done. **34** And some among the multitude cried one thing and some another. So when he could not ascertain the truth because of the tumult, he commanded him to be taken into the barracks. **35** When he reached the stairs, he had to be carried by the soldiers because of the violence of the mob. **36** For the multitude of the people followed after, crying out, "Away with him!" **37** Then as Paul was about to be led into the barracks, he said to the commander, "May I speak to you?" He replied, "Can you speak Greek? **38** Are you not the Egyptian who some time ago stirred up a rebellion and led the four thousand assassins out into the wilderness?" **39** But Paul said, "I am a Jew from Tarsus, in Cilicia, a citizen of no mean city; and I implore you, permit me to speak to the people." **40** So when he had given him permission, Paul stood on the stairs and motioned with his hand to the people. And when there was a great silence, he spoke to them in the Hebrew language, saying, **1** "Brethren and fathers, hear my defense before you now." **2** And when they heard that he spoke to them in the Hebrew language, they kept all the more silent. Then he said: **3** "I am indeed a Jew, born in Tarsus of Cilicia, but brought up in this city at the feet of Gamaliel, taught according to the strictness of our fathers' law, and was zealous toward God as you all are today. **4** I persecuted this Way to the death, binding and delivering into prisons both men and women, **5** as also the high priest bears me witness, and all the council of the elders, from whom I also received letters to the brethren, and went to Damascus to bring in chains even those who were there to Jerusalem to be punished. **6** Now it happened, as I journeyed and came near Damascus at about noon, suddenly a great light from heaven shone around me. **7** And I fell to the ground and heard a voice saying to me, 'Saul, Saul, why are you persecuting Me?' **8** So I answered, 'Who are You, Lord?' And He said to me, 'I am Jesus of Nazareth, whom you are persecuting.' **9** And those who were with me indeed saw the light and were afraid, but they did not hear the voice of Him who spoke to me. **10** So I said, 'What shall I do, Lord?' And the Lord said to me, 'Arise and go into Damascus, and there you will be told all things which are appointed for you to do.' **11** And since I could not see for the glory of that light, being led by the hand of those who were with me, I came into Damascus. **12** Then a certain Ananias, a devout man according to the law, having a good testimony with all the Jews who dwelt there, **13** came to me; and he stood and said to me, 'Brother Saul, receive your sight.' And at that same hour I looked up at him. **14** Then he said, 'The God of our fathers has chosen you that you should know His will, and see the Just One, and hear the voice of His mouth. **15** For you will be His witness to all men of what you have seen and heard. **16** And now why are you waiting? Arise and be baptized, and wash away your sins, calling on the name of the Lord.' **17** Now it happened, when I returned to Jerusalem and was praying in the temple, that I was in a trance **18** and saw Him saying to me, 'Make haste and get out of Jerusalem quickly, for they will not receive your testimony concerning Me.' **19** So I said, 'Lord, they know that in every synagogue I imprisoned and beat those who believe on You. **20** And when the blood of Your martyr Stephen was shed, I also was standing by consenting to his death, and guarding the clothes of those who were killing him.' **21** Then He said to me, 'Depart, for I will send you far from here to the Gentiles.' " **22** And they listened to him until this word, and then they raised their voices and said, "Away with such a fellow from the earth, for he is not fit to live!" **23** Then, as they cried out and tore off their clothes and threw dust into the air.

The plan hatched in order to reassure the Jewish Christians did not reassure non-Christian Jews. They expressed zeal for the law and traditions but were quite willing to descend into a mob frenzy. The irony was that their stated objective of upholding the law was nullified by the attempted lawless lynching of Paul.

They displayed acts of the sinful nature, which include hatred, contentions jealousy and outbursts of wrath. (Gal 5: 19-21)

The law of God is upheld by exhibiting the fruits of the Spirit, of which they seemed to know little:

But the fruit of the Spirit is love, joy, peace, longsuffering, kindness, goodness, faithfulness, gentleness, self-control. Against such there is no law. (Gal 5: 22- 23)

It took an intervention by a pagan force of Roman soldiers to prevent loss of life. Just as the crowd over twenty years earlier had shouted, "Crucify Him," about the Son of God, so they cried, "Away with such a fellow," about His servant. Through all of this, Paul remained silent. At that stage reasoning with the mob would have been pointless. Opposition to Christ of this type rarely changes its colours. Today, new atheists are becoming even more strident and open in their outbursts against God and Christianity.

Paul was bound with chains, a fulfilment of the prophecy received in Caesarea. From then on Paul would remain a prisoner till the end of Acts. Although the great apostle and communicator of the faith was bound, the progress of the gospel was not. Throughout this lack of freedom and privation, Paul never lost his composure and confidence in God. Whilst in prison, he wrote:

Just as it is right for me to think this of you all, because I have you in my heart, inasmuch as both in my chains and in the defence and confirmation of the gospel, you all are partakers with me of grace. For God is my witness, how greatly I long for you all with the affection of Jesus Christ. (Phil 1: 7-8)

Moreover, Paul maintained a grip of the situation and knowledge of language. To the commander's surprise he spoke in polished Greek, and then he was allowed to speak to the crowd in Aramaic. At this point, the crowd was hushed and Paul began his first defence as a prisoner.

Paul's defence consisted of two main points. The first point was that he was a loyal, true Jew, and that his experience was in continuity with the Messianic hope. Jesus was the "Just one," which was a Messianic title. The second point was that he had received instructions from the Lord, through a vision to go to the Gentiles. Before moving on to the reaction to that last statement, it would be profitable to pause and digress a little concerning two particular phrases in the speech.

Paul spoke about Jesus as the "Just (or Righteous) One" (v 14). Peter referred to this in his second sermon in chapter three of Acts. The term has a lot more significance for us than we might at first realise. Jeremiah used the term, "The Lord our Righteousness"

(Jeremiah 23: 6 and 33:16), and these words have been the text of many a sermon. The wonderful teaching behind these words is that when we become Christians, not only do we ask Christ into our hearts and lives, we put Him on like a large overcoat. From that time of initiation, when God looks at us, He does not declare us as we are, imperfect, fault-prone sinners but as people covered or enveloped in the righteousness of Christ. He sees Christ's righteousness around and on us. That is our unfathomable status. Of course, we still make mistakes and we still have a tendency to sin, as we see in Acts, and the rest of the Bible, but we also have this new standing before God. Paul explained this in his epistles to the Romans and Corinthians. (Rom 3: 21-22, 1 Cor 1:30) At his conversion, Paul must have been profoundly ridden with guilt, in view of his previous history of violent persecution towards God's people. The symbol of baptism and the washing away of sins must have been very significant for him. (v 16) He knew in his heart that he was truly forgiven and truly cleansed. The Bible teaches us that we are, in fact, washed by the shed blood of Christ on the cross.

But if we walk in the light as He is in the light, we have fellowship with one another, and the blood of Jesus Christ His Son cleanses us from all sin. (1 John 1: 7)

The reaction of the crowd displayed their utter hatred for the Gentiles, and for Paul himself. Pray to God that we do not display similar contempt for other peoples and individuals.

Acts 22:24-23:10

24 The commander ordered him to be brought into the barracks, and said that he should be examined under scourging, so that he might know why they shouted so against him. **25** And as they bound him with thongs, Paul said to the centurion who stood by, "Is it lawful for you to scourge a man who is a Roman, and uncondemned?" **26** When the centurion heard that, he went and told the commander, saying, "Take care what you do, for this man is a Roman." **27** Then the commander came and said to him, "Tell me, are you a Roman?" He said, "Yes." **28** The commander answered, "With a large sum I obtained this citizenship." And Paul said, "But I was born a citizen." **29** Then immediately those who were about to examine him withdrew from him; and the commander was also afraid after he found out that he was a Roman, and because he had bound him. **30** The next day, because he wanted to know for certain why he was accused by the Jews, he released him from his bonds, and commanded the chief priests and all their council to appear, and brought Paul down and set him before them.

1 Then Paul, looking earnestly at the council, said, "Men and brethren, I have lived in all good conscience before God until this day." **2** And the high priest Ananias commanded those who stood by him to strike him on the mouth. **3** Then Paul said to him, "God will strike you, you whitewashed wall! For you sit to judge me according to the law, and do you command me to be struck contrary to the law?" **4** And those who stood by said, "Do you revile God's high priest? **5** Then Paul said, "I did not know, brethren, that he was the high priest; for it is written, 'You shall not speak evil of a ruler of your people.' " **6** But when Paul perceived that one part were Sadducees and the other Pharisees, he cried out in the council, "Men and brethren, I am a Pharisee, the son of a Pharisee; concerning the hope and resurrection of the dead I am being judged!" **7** And when he had said this, a dissension arose between the Pharisees and the Sadducees; and the assembly was divided. **8** For Sadducees say that there is no resurrection--and no angel or spirit; but the Pharisees confess both. **9** Then there arose a loud outcry. And the scribes of the Pharisees' party arose and protested, saying, "We find no evil in this man; but if a spirit or an angel has spoken to him, let us not fight against God." **10** Now when there arose a great dissension, the commander, fearing lest Paul might be pulled to pieces by them, commanded the soldiers to go down and take him by force from among them, and bring him into the barracks.

The unrest and noise of the crowds prompted some decisive action by the Roman commander and this indicates the lengths to which authorities will go to obtain a result both agreeable to the masses and to their superiors. The logic was that Paul must have been guilty of some grave crime. Therefore they were quite prepared to use torture to obtain information, even though the material derived by such methods is usually unreliable. Even today, democratic nations have used torture and unusual punishment on those suspected of terrorist and other crimes.

Clearly, in Paul's case the centurion must have still thought that Paul may have been involved in a local uprising or similar incident. The deplorable use of flogging could and often did lead to the death of the victim. Paul had already suffered numerous beatings during his Christian ministry. On this occasion he used his last means of defence, namely his Roman citizenship. To lie about such a claim could have led to the death penalty.

The flogging of a Roman citizen without due legal process was a serious offence, and consequently, the commander and the questioners backtracked rapidly.

The fact remained that if Paul had not been a Roman citizen, then he would have suffered an early death from his captors, such was the value placed on the lives of many subjects of the Roman Empire. What value do we put on human life? God values and loves us so much that He was prepared to send His Son to die for us. We should seek to love others in some way to reflect the love He has for us, and them.

The commander wanted to have information, and at last sought to obtain it in a proper fashion before the assembly of the Sanhedrin.

In spite of all that had gone before, the rejection, the cruelty and many persecutions, Paul began his evidence by use of the word, "Brethren". These are people who were his kinsmen, and whom he longed to become believers:

I have great sorrow and continual grief in my heart. For I could wish that I myself were accursed from Christ for my brethren, my countrymen according to the flesh, who are Israelites, to whom pertain the adoption, the glory, the covenants, the giving of the law, the service of God, and the promises (Rom 9: 2-4)

We should have a special place in our hearts and prayers for the Jewish people, as those out of their number continue to come to faith in Jesus the Messiah, Lord and Saviour.

The order by the chief priest to strike Paul was typical of the man. Ananias, who had been manipulated into his position by Herod, behaved more like a Mafia boss than a pious high priest. He extorted money from his fellow priests and was quite prepared to murder people in the maintenance of his power. Not long after, he was deposed, and assassinated.

Although Paul apologized for his stricture against Ananias, the irony is that the high priest indeed was "a whitewashed wall".

There is a lesson here that we too, at times, should be prepared to apologise when taken to task by a rebuke. Many commentators have compared Paul's initial response to the blow on his face, to that Jesus received when in front of the high priest:

And when He had said these things, one of the officers who stood by struck Jesus with the palm of his hand, saying, "Do You answer the high priest like that?" Jesus answered him, "If I have spoken evil, bear witness of the evil; but if well, why do you strike Me?" (John 18: 22-23)

Paul then tried to split two groups within first century Judaism. The success of his address was marked by such a violent argument between the Pharisees and the Sadducees that it seemed that Paul's life was once more in danger. It speaks volumes about the misdirected zeal of those peoples at that time:

For I bear them witness that they have a zeal for God, but not according to knowledge. For they being ignorant of God's righteousness, and seeking to establish their own righteousness, have not submitted to the righteousness of God (Rom 10: 2-3)

The Roman authority had to intervene again to prevent loss of life.

Acts 23:11-24

11 But the following night the Lord stood by him and said, "Be of good cheer, Paul; for as you have testified for Me in Jerusalem, so you must also bear witness at Rome." 12 And when it was day, some of the Jews banded together and bound themselves under an oath, saying that they would neither eat nor drink till they had killed Paul. 13 Now there were more than forty who had formed this conspiracy. 14 They came to the chief priests and elders, and said, "We have bound ourselves under a great oath that we will eat nothing until we have killed Paul 15 Now you, therefore, together with the council, suggest to the commander that he be brought down to you tomorrow, as though you were going to make further inquiries concerning him; but we are ready to kill him before he comes near." 16 So when Paul's sister's son heard of their ambush, he went and entered the barracks and told Paul. 17 Then Paul called one of the centurions to him and said, "Take this young man to the commander, for he has something to tell him." 18 So he took him and brought him to the commander and said, "Paul the prisoner called me to him and asked me to bring this young man to you. He has something to say to you." 19 Then the commander took him by the hand, went aside and asked privately, "What is it that you have to tell me? 20 And he said, "The Jews have agreed to ask that you bring Paul down to the council tomorrow, as though they were going to inquire more fully about him. 21 But do not yield to them, for more than forty of them lie in wait for him, men who have bound themselves by an oath that they will neither eat nor drink till they have killed him; and now they are ready, waiting for the promise from you. 22 So the commander let the young man depart, and commanded him, "Tell no one that you have revealed these things to me." 23 And he called for two centurions, saying, "Prepare two hundred soldiers, seventy horsemen, and two hundred spearmen to go to Caesarea at the third hour of the night; 24 and provide mounts to set Paul on, and bring him safely to Felix the governor."

Paul was at another crisis in his life and as on previous occasions, this was accompanied by a profound spiritual experience. The Lord Jesus appeared to him. The Lord also had been unlawfully tried. Although He is the King of kings, He did not have the benefit of Roman citizenship. He was flogged and crucified so that we could be forgiven and made citizens of a far nobler place, the kingdom of God.

Paul's service was not yet over, he was going to testify and share the gospel in Rome. Whatever crisis we face we can always remember our Lord's gentle words to the disciples, "Fear not!" We may not understand why and how but God's purposes always come to fruition.

The failure of the Sanhedrin to arrive at a decision of guilt, led a radicalised group to create a plot to kill Paul. Such was their fanaticism that they sealed their plot with an oath.

The party of the Zealots hated the Roman occupiers and all that they represented as Gentiles. They could not tolerate the Christian mission to the Gentiles. Some years later they led two revolts against Roman rule, which resulted in a brutal response. The temple and many towns and villages were utterly destroyed. Hundreds of thousands were killed and the land was virtually de-populated. The province's name changed from Judaea to Syria Palaestina, from which we have the name Palestine.

The discovery of the plot by Paul's nephew and the advice by his sister may imply that they also were believers. We do not know when they became Christians, but it is always a great joy when family members come to faith. Conversely, it is a sadness when relatives remain unconvinced, as happened to a number of Old Testament prophets, among them, Samuel and Job. Whatever the spiritual position of our relatives; never give up on kindness, never give up on prayer. There are instances of family coming to faith after many years of persistent and faithful prayer. There are also instances when no such change of heart has ever taken place. It is a matter that is in God's hands.

Paul's nephew's warning of a plot led to a quick response by the Roman commander. The prisoner would be transferred to the secure Mediterranean city of Caesarea. The rapid exit from Jerusalem accompanied by a large detachment of troops indicated the volatile political and military situation at that time.

As Paul travelled along the road to the coast, he was leaving

Jerusalem for the last time. It was the city where Paul had been a student and a young activist lawyer. It was where he had witnessed the stoning of Stephen. After his conversion, it was the place where Barnabas had helped him and introduced him to the apostles and where he too had testified about Jesus. It was the site of the great Jerusalem council where he had spoken concerning the conversion of the Gentiles. In the last few days, it was a place of anger and violence, and where he was close to death at the hands of a mob. The city that should have been so much more of a blessing to the world, would soon, in a few years, be surrounded by armies.

Years before, when Jesus came near the city, He wept:

Now as He drew near, He saw the city and wept over it, saying, "If you had known, even you, especially in this your day, the things that make for your peace! But now they are hidden from your eyes." (Luke 19: 41-42)

Down the centuries Jerusalem has been the focus of world attention and conflict and remains so to this day. Some have described it as a flashpoint, which could herald a dreadful war in the Middle- East. The Bible urges us to pray for the peace of Jerusalem. (Ps 122: 6)

Acts 23:25-24:27

25 He wrote a letter in the following manner: **26** Claudius Lysias, To the most excellent governor Felix: Greetings. **27** This man was seized by the Jews and was about to be killed by them. Coming with the troops I rescued him, having learned that he was a Roman. **28** And when I wanted to know the reason they accused him, I brought him before their council. **29** I found out that he was accused concerning questions of their law, but had nothing charged against him deserving of death or chains. **30** And when it was told me that the Jews lay in wait for the man, I sent him immediately to you, and also commanded his accusers to state before you the charges against him. Farewell. **31** Then the soldiers, as they were commanded, took Paul and brought him by night to Antipatris. **32** The next day they left the horsemen to go on with him, and returned to the barracks. **33** When they came to Caesarea and had delivered the letter to the governor, they also presented Paul to him. **34** And when the governor had read it, he asked what province he was from. And when he understood that he was from Cilicia, **35** he said, "I will hear you when your accusers also have come." And he commanded him to be kept in Herod's Praetorium.

1 Now after five days Ananias the high priest came down with the elders and a certain orator named Tertullus. These gave evidence to the governor against Paul. **2** And when he was called upon, Tertullus began his accusation, saying: "Seeing that through you we enjoy great peace, and prosperity is being brought to this nation by your foresight, **3** we accept it always and in all places, most noble Felix, with all thankfulness. **4** Nevertheless, not to be tedious to you any further, I beg you to hear, by your courtesy, a few words from us. **5** For we have found this man a plague, a creator of dissension among all the Jews throughout the world, and a ringleader of the sect of the Nazarenes. **6** He even tried to profane the temple, and we seized him, and wanted to judge him according to our law. **7** But the commander Lysias came by and with great violence took him out of our hands, **8** commanding his accusers to come to you. By examining him yourself you may ascertain all these things of which we accuse him." **9** And the Jews also assented, maintaining that these things were so. **10** Then Paul, after the governor had nodded to him to speak, answered: "Inasmuch as I know that you have been for many years a judge of this nation, I do the more cheerfully answer for myself, **11** because you may ascertain that it is no more than twelve days since I went up to Jerusalem to worship. **12** And they neither found me in the temple disputing with anyone nor inciting the crowd, either in the synagogues or in the city. **13** Nor can they prove the things of which they now accuse me. **14** But this I confess to you, that according to the Way which they call a sect, so I worship the God of my fathers, believing all things which are written in the Law and in the Prophets. **15** I have hope in God, which they themselves also accept, that there will be a resurrection of the dead, both of the just and the unjust. **16** This being so, I myself always strive to have a conscience without offense toward God and men. **17** Now after many years I came to bring alms and offerings to my nation, **18** in the midst of which some Jews from Asia found me purified in the temple, neither with a mob nor with tumult. **19** They ought to have been here before you to object if they had anything against me. **20** Or else let those who are here themselves say if they found any wrongdoing in me while I stood before the council, **21** unless it is for this one statement which I cried out, standing among them, 'Concerning the resurrection of the dead I am being judged by you this day.' " **22** But when Felix heard these things, having more accurate knowledge of the Way, he adjourned the proceedings and said, "When Lysias the commander comes down, I will make a decision on your case." **23** So he commanded the centurion to keep Paul and to let him have liberty, and told him not to forbid any of his friends to provide for or visit him. **24** And after some days, when Felix came with his wife Drusilla, who was Jewish, he sent for Paul and heard him concerning the faith in Christ. **25** Now as he reasoned about righteousness, self-control, and the judgment to come, Felix was afraid and answered, "Go away for now; when I have a convenient time I will call for you." **26** Meanwhile he also hoped that money would be given him by Paul, that he might release him. Therefore he sent for him more often and conversed with him. **27** But after two years Porcius Festus succeeded Felix; and Felix, wanting to do the Jews a favor, left Paul bound.

The letter that Claudius Lysias wrote to the governor Felix is an example of military brevity and manipulation of the facts. Such letters have their representatives to this day.

He attempted to place himself in a good position by saying that he had saved Paul from the crowd because his prisoner was a Roman citizen. In fact Paul was stretched out, and about to be flogged by his own soldiers, before Lysias had learnt of his Roman citizenship. He wanted to assure his governor that he had acted properly, efficiently and judiciously in his management of the whole affair. Christians should always take care to tell the truth. It is always tempting to tell half-truths to make us appear in a good light, something that we should avoid.

Felix clearly wanted to have the whole thing settled as soon as possible. He was of slave origins and had risen to the position of governor under Emperor Claudius. He was known for his brutality in dealing with rebellion, and his "wandering eyes", since he married three queens in succession. Later he was ordered to return to Rome in disgrace, where he was fortunate not to be a victim of the death penalty.

The trial before Felix indicated the dilemma that Felix and later judges faced. Should they appease the Jewish authorities and hand Paul over to certain death, or should they observe due process of law, of which the Romans were so proud, and find the defendant not guilty?

The elderly Ananias made the hundred-kilometre journey to Caesarea, accompanied by colleagues and a lawyer familiar with Roman legal procedure. Their accusations against Paul were groundless, and it is worth taking note of the skill Paul employed to deal with them.

After Tertullus began with the usual dose of flattery, the first accusation was that Paul stirred up riots all over the world. This was a totally inaccurate interpretation of the facts, since it was the Jews themselves that had stirred up the crowds. Paul did not reply directly to that but confined himself only to the land of Felix's jurisdiction. The prosecuting lawyer tried to accuse Paul of desecrating the temple. Wrong again! Paul was a Jew, and only accompanied by Jews on an act of worship. He spoke to no-one. Trouble only arose when some Greek Jews from the province of Asia spotted him, and made false accusations that he had brought a Gentile into the temple.

Paul did admit that he was a follower of Jesus, but insisted that he worshipped, "The God of our Fathers."

Paul's skill was and is not usual, but Jesus does promise that when we get into difficult situations on account of Him, He will give us the words to say:

But when they deliver you up, do not worry about how or what you should speak. For it will be given to you in that hour what you should speak; for it is not you who speak, but the Spirit of your Father who speaks in you. (Matt 10: 19-20)

This is a wonderful promise and comfort to those undergoing the pressures of persecution.

Felix adjourned the trial, and this was followed by two notable events, which arose at subsequent hearings.

The first is the fact that Paul spoke of righteousness, self-control, and judgement to come. Felix was afraid. One translation puts it that he trembled. I have never heard of an incident in the long legal history of the world, when a defendant, except perhaps in the instance of Mafia-organised crime, caused a judge to be afraid and tremble. Although Felix had all the power and might of Rome behind him, he was rightly disturbed by the prospect of standing before the judgement seat of God. Sadly, these emotions did not bring him or his wife, Drusilla, to a state of repentance and faith in Christ.

Secondly, Felix had further private conversations but was corrupt and expected a bribe. He is reminiscent of one of his regional predecessors, Herod Antipas, who enjoyed conversations with John the Baptist. Although these men may have been fascinated by the religion of Paul and John, they were unmoved spiritually, and remained in their wickedness. We should always be sensitive to our consciences and moved by the promptings of the Holy Spirit. Paul was held in custody without any conclusion by the court for two years. He lived by faith in the Son of God and had the consolation, support and kindness of Christian friends.

Acts 25:1-22

1 Now when Festus had come to the province, after three days he went up from Caesarea to Jerusalem. 2 Then the high priest and the chief men of the Jews informed him against Paul; and they petitioned him, 3 asking a favor against him, that he would summon him to Jerusalem--while they lay in ambush along the road to kill him. 4 But Festus answered that Paul should be kept at Caesarea, and that he himself was going there shortly. 5 "Therefore," he said, "let those who have authority among you go down with me and accuse this man, to see if there is any fault in him." 6 And when he had remained among them more than ten days, he went down to Caesarea. And the next day, sitting on the judgment seat, he commanded Paul to be brought. 7 When he had come, the Jews who had come down from Jerusalem stood about and laid many serious complaints against Paul, which they could not prove, 8 while he answered for himself, "Neither against the law of the Jews, nor against the temple, nor against Caesar have I offended in anything at all." 9 But Festus, wanting to do the Jews a favor, answered Paul and said, "Are you willing to go up to Jerusalem and there be judged before me concerning these things?" 10 So Paul said, "I stand at Caesar's judgment seat, where I ought to be judged. To the Jews I have done no wrong, as you very well know. 11 For if I am an offender, or have committed anything deserving of death, I do not object to dying; but if there is nothing in these things of which these men accuse me, no one can deliver me to them. I appeal to Caesar." 12 Then Festus, when he had conferred with the council, answered, "You have appealed to Caesar? To Caesar you shall go!" 13 And after some days King Agrippa and Bernice came to Caesarea to greet Festus. 14 When they had been there many days, Festus laid Paul's case before the king, saying: "There is a certain man left a prisoner by Felix, 15 about whom the chief priests and the elders of the Jews informed me, when I was in Jerusalem, asking for a judgment against him. 16 To them I answered, 'It is not the custom of the Romans to deliver any man to destruction before the accused meets the accusers face to face, and has opportunity to answer for himself concerning the charge against him.' 17 Therefore when they had come together, without any delay, the next day I sat on the judgment seat and commanded the man to be brought in. 18 When the accusers stood up, they brought no accusation against him of such things as I supposed, 19 but had some questions against him about their own religion and about a certain Jesus, who had died, whom Paul

affirmed to be alive. **20** And because I was uncertain of such questions, I asked whether he was willing to go to Jerusalem and there be judged concerning these matters. **21** But when Paul appealed to be reserved for the decision of Augustus, I commanded him to be kept till I could send him to Caesar." **22** Then Agrippa said to Festus, "I also would like to hear the man myself." "Tomorrow," he said, "you shall hear him."

The replacement of Felix by Festus brought in a much more capable and efficient administrator, who was known for his honesty and integrity. He must have been irritated by the backlog of unfinished business left by his predecessor. One such item was the case brought against Paul. His fact-finding mission to Jerusalem over this and other matters made clear the fanaticism and hatred against Paul by his accusers. In spite of all this and the two years in custody, Paul had no bitterness or self-pity that would have marked most of us. He was one who took up his cross daily, without resentment, but with a love for his Lord, who loved him first. He still had an ambition in his heart to take the gospel to Rome and beyond.

Festus the politician invited Paul's accusers to Caesarea and another hearing was convened. Once again, they were unable to prove their charges, and Paul stood by his defence that he had done no wrong against the law or the temple. However, the presence of Festus, brought the authority and rule of Caesar into the proceedings. Paul insisted that he had done nothing wrong against Caesar either. He was prepared to die if he was guilty of any capital crime. Festus knew that Paul was not guilty of a capital offence, but he did not want to anger the Jews of Jerusalem by releasing him there and then.

Festus offered yet another trial in Jerusalem. Surely that would clear the whole matter, and deal with this nagging and, to him, irrelevant problem. Paul kept his wits about him and declined the proposal. There would be no safety in Jerusalem. So he appealed to the highest court in the empire, he appealed to Caesar.

Festus after consultation agreed. Festus still had a lingering doubt that Rome would be irritated by this seemingly unnecessary case. So he thought he would gain the backing of a neighbouring ruler, King Herod Agrippa the Second, a puppet king installed by Caesar. The Herods were a dynasty of kings, known for their brutality. Agrippa's Father was responsible for the death of James the apostle. However, this Herod did know something about religion. He would have heard about this new 'sect', which most people regarded as a nuisance.

Festus's short summary of the case is clear and accurate. However, he typifies so many. There are vast numbers in the West who have decided to have no interest in God, Christianity, or the deep issues of life. There are people who have a sense of honesty and integrity, and yet they keep well away from religion, and Christianity in particular. They become irritated by invitations to church. They refuse to discuss the matters around death, or bereavement and find any appeal to their consciences too much of a challenge. Festus talked about the resurrection of "a certain Jesus", without any attempt to look into it. If he discovered the proof and truth of it, then his lifestyle and whole world-view would have to change.

Jesus was right when He said that people would remain in unbelief, even though one were to rise from the dead. (Luke 16:31)

In the past, they may have looked on Christianity with a benign indifference. But more recently, many construct a false image of Christianity as being out-of-date, responsible for wars, discrimination, wife and child abuse, slavery, intolerance, and all kinds of other problems in our society.

However, the reply to such thinking was the life and example of such a man who stood in front of Festus, the apostle Paul. Although persuasion and sermons bring people to Christ, many more come through the reading of Scripture and the witness and demeanour of friends, family and colleagues. J. C. Ryle said that that these types of witness are arrows from God's own quiver, and will often pierce hearts, which have not been touched by the most eloquent sermon.

Acts 25:23-26:11

23 So the next day, when Agrippa and Bernice had come with great pomp, and had entered the auditorium with the commanders and the prominent men of the city, at Festus' command Paul was brought in. 24 And Festus said: "King Agrippa and all the men who are here present with us, you see this man about whom the whole assembly of the Jews petitioned me, both at Jerusalem and here, crying out that he was not fit to live any longer. 25 But when I found that he had committed nothing deserving of death, and that he himself had appealed to Augustus, I decided to send him. 26 I have nothing certain to write to my lord concerning him. Therefore I have brought him out before you, and especially before you, King Agrippa, so that after the examination has taken place I may have something to write. 27 For it seems to me unreasonable to send a prisoner and not to specify the charges against him.

1 Then Agrippa said to Paul, "You are permitted to speak for yourself." So Paul stretched out his hand and answered for himself: 2 "I think myself happy, King Agrippa, because today I shall answer for myself before you concerning all the things of which I am accused by the Jews, 3 especially because you are expert in all customs and questions which have to do with the Jews. Therefore I beg you to hear me patiently. 4 My manner of life from my youth, which was spent from the beginning among my own nation at Jerusalem, all the Jews know. 5 They knew me from the first, if they were willing to testify, that according to the strictest sect of our religion I lived a Pharisee. 6 And now I stand and am judged for the hope of the promise made by God to our fathers. 7 To this promise our twelve tribes, earnestly serving God night and day, hope to attain. For this hope's sake, King Agrippa, I am accused by the Jews. 8 Why should it be thought incredible by you that God raises the dead? 9 Indeed, I myself thought I must do many things contrary to the name of Jesus of Nazareth. 10 This I also did in Jerusalem, and many of the saints I shut up in prison, having received authority from the chief priests; and when they were put to death, I cast my vote against them. 11 And I punished them often in every synagogue and compelled them to blaspheme; and being exceedingly enraged against them, I persecuted them even to foreign cities.

The next day began with all the pomp and performance that signifies and promotes the reality as well as the illusion of worldly power. The two rulers, Bernice and all the officials were in place. Then the ordinarily dressed, chained, lone, scarred but not scared representative of the King of kings was brought in.

Festus was faced with a number of problems.

Firstly, even after two years of custody, the whole Jewish community in Jerusalem and Caesarea were shouting for Paul's death. To Festus, Paul had done nothing worthy of death or imprisonment. Like so many politicians before or since, should he do what the crowds want, or should he do what he believed to be right? Like so many politicians, his way out was to pass the problem to another, namely upward to Caesar.

Secondly, however, he was at a loss as to what to write in the accompanying letter. He would look stupid, since he was unable to list any charges that would be of interest or significance to the emperor. This is where Agrippa's experience and understanding would come in. We should pray that our politicians should not make merely expedient decisions, but wise ones.

Paul was then invited to speak. After two years, Paul had lost none of his style. He drew attention to what he was about to say by raising his hand, a gesture to be repeated by thousands of preachers in subsequent centuries. Paul preached not only with his mouth but also with his whole being.

He made the customary compliments to the judge, without the excessive flattery as used in the previous chapter by Tertullus when standing before Felix. Then for the third time in Acts, we have an account of Paul's conversion.

The three descriptions signify the importance of the event

There is no one too bad who cannot come to Christ. We all have to make a conscious decision to turn to Christ. Although promises may be made on our behalf as infants, ultimately promises to follow Christ are ours alone.

The first part of Paul's testimony was about his life before his conversion, and is put there to establish his credentials, firstly as an orthodox Jew, and a member of Judaism's strictest sect, the Pharisees. Secondly, his hope is that expressed in the Hebrew

Scriptures, namely the resurrection of the dead. This was something that most of his hearers rejected. It is one which we would naturally reject except for the testimony of the witnesses and experience of the resurrection of Jesus.

Then Paul moved on to his actions, which must have given him hurt, even after all those years.

He was the leader of a phase of persecution, which was hard-hitting and widespread. He singled out believers to recant their faith, and shared responsibility for passing the death penalty on others. This, as we have already seen, caused a dispersion of the believers and the poverty of many. It was a custom to throw believers out of the synagogue. Not only were they denied a place of worship, the expulsion and rejection caused many to lose their means of livelihood. It was an example how evil could seep into a misplaced religious fanaticism. No doubt, this acquired poverty by the Messianic believers in Judaea was one of the reasons that Paul was so willing to make collections for them.

Whilst we should be on fire for God, true Godly fire makes a person patient, understanding and kind. True Christians may be persecuted but they should not be persecutors! The Apostle Peter made these remarks about persecution:

But even if you should suffer for righteousness' sake, you are blessed. "And do not be afraid of their threats, nor be troubled." But sanctify the Lord God in your hearts, and always be ready to give a defense to everyone who asks you a reason for the hope that is in you, with meekness and fear; (1 Pet 3: 14-15)

Acts 26:12-18

12 "While thus occupied, as I journeyed to Damascus with authority and commission from the chief priests, 13 at midday, O king, along the road I saw a light from heaven, brighter than the sun, shining around me and those who journeyed with me. 14 And when we all had fallen to the ground, I heard a voice speaking to me and saying in the Hebrew language, 'Saul, Saul, why are you persecuting Me? It is hard for you to kick against the goads.' 15 So I said, 'Who are You, Lord?' And He said, 'I am Jesus, whom you are persecuting. 16 But rise and stand on your feet; for I have appeared to you for this purpose, to make you a minister and a witness both of the things which you have seen and of the things which I will yet reveal to you. 17 I will deliver you from the Jewish people, as well as from the Gentiles, to whom I now send you, 18 to open their eyes, in order to turn them from darkness to light, and from the power of Satan to God, that they may receive forgiveness of sins and an inheritance among those who are sanctified by faith in Me.'

This third account of Paul's conversion includes a reference to a bright light and the effects on Paul and also his companions. There is no description of subsequent events, namely the ministry of Ananias and his baptism. However, Paul's commission as a servant and witness is spelt out more clearly.

It is intriguing to note that Paul would be rescued from his own people and the Gentiles. Not only would he survive severe persecutions at the hands of his fellow countrymen, but perhaps it also included rescue from his own nationalist prejudices, in particular those he had towards the Gentiles. We all have prejudices, which we need to ask Christ to heal.

In this passage we are brought into a deeper understanding of Paul's motivation, which are the words of Jesus himself.

First of all, we see that the natural state of a world without Christ is one of darkness. People live in darkness and are also blind (v 18).

They do not appreciate how dark it is until the light is switched on. Festus and millions living in the world today are under that misapprehension. They do not realise the reality of sin. Their talk is of bad choices and inappropriate behaviour. There is a refusal to believe that there is a principle of me first that is so ingrained in all of us that it pervades all that we do. Furthermore, they have difficulty over the way we should go because they turn their backs on God's way and God's truth. Moreover, we all have a tendency to turn away from the light of Christ, which should attract us. Such is the power of darkness:

And this is the condemnation, that the light has come into the world, and men loved darkness rather than light, because their deeds were evil. For everyone practicing evil hates the light and does not come to the light, lest his deeds should be exposed. (John 3: 19-20)

Secondly, we see that people without Christ are under the power of Satan. In Acts, and in the Gospels there are some obvious bizarre presentations of demon possession. What is not so obvious is that Satan, who masquerades as an angel of light, has blinded the eyes of millions of 'nice' people, nice people who believe that they have no need of God.

Paul's task was to be a witness so that God could open the eyes of the spiritually blind in order to see their state of sin and need. He was to help people, who under the impulse of the Holy Sprit could turn from darkness to the beautiful, guiding and attractive light of Christ. Peter put the change in this way:

No longer would they be under the power of Satan but under the wise, gentle and loving power of God.

The object of this was and still is that people should know and receive forgiveness of sins. This forgiveness comes by means of the cross of Christ. Paul by the time of this trial had already written:

But God demonstrates His own love toward us, in that while we were still sinners, Christ died for us. Much more then, having now been justified by His blood, we shall be saved from wrath through Him. (Rom 5: 8-9)

Included with forgiveness is a life-journey of transformation in a community of those who seek to do God's will and become more like Christ. Although glaring weaknesses would persist, as shown in the letter to the Corinthians, the path would be in the right direction. Peter described the change very cogently:

But you are a chosen generation, a royal priesthood, a holy nation, His own special people, that you may proclaim the praises of Him who called you out of darkness into His marvelous light; who once were not a people but are now the people of God, who had not obtained mercy but now have obtained mercy. (1 Pet 2: 9-10)

This is the journey of faith in Christ that would touch the hearts of millions.

Acts 26:19-32

19 "Therefore, King Agrippa, I was not disobedient to the heavenly vision, **20** but declared first to those in Damascus and in Jerusalem, and throughout all the region of Judea, and then to the Gentiles, that they should repent, turn to God, and do works befitting repentance. **21** For these reasons the Jews seized me in the temple and tried to kill me. **22** Therefore, having obtained help from God, to this day I stand, witnessing both to small and great, saying no other things than those which the prophets and Moses said would come-- **23** that the Christ would suffer, that He would be the first to rise from the dead, and would proclaim light to the Jewish people and to the Gentiles." **24** Now as he thus made his defense, Festus said with a loud voice, "Paul, you are beside yourself! Much learning is driving you mad!" **25** But he said, "I am not mad, most noble Festus, but speak the words of truth and reason. **26** For the king, before whom I also speak freely, knows these things; for I am convinced that none of these things escapes his attention, since this thing was not done in a corner. **27** King Agrippa, do you believe the prophets? I know that you do believe." **28** Then Agrippa said to Paul, "You almost persuade me to become a Christian." **29** And Paul said, "I would to God that not only you, but also all who hear me today, might become both almost and altogether such as I am, except for these chains." **30** When he had said these things, the king stood up, as well as the governor and Bernice and those who sat with them; **31** and when they had gone aside, they talked among themselves, saying, "This man is doing nothing deserving of death or chains." **32** Then Agrippa said to Festus, "This man might have been set free if he had not appealed to Caesar."

Paul knew that Agrippa had some knowledge of Jewish matters and Christianity. He was himself part Jewish and had been brought up in the court of Claudius Caesar. Therefore, he would not have been antagonistic to ministry amongst the Gentiles. Once again, Paul stated his mission to the Gentiles - that they should turn to God in true repentance.

Here we should take the opportunity to mark the difference between true repentance and saying sorry with some form of regret. Godly sorrow is an experience of divine grace that leads to true repentance towards God. The result leads to forgiveness and the intention to go in a different direction in obedience to God. Worldly sorrow is a self-centred sorrow over actions, failures and the resulting consequences. It is painful but brings about no lasting change towards God. (2 Cor 7: 10)

Paul then appealed to the authority of the Old Testament. Moses and the prophets testified about all that would happen to Jesus, including the cross and resurrection. Moses's reference to the Messiah is found in the book of Deuteronomy:

The Lord your God will raise up for you a Prophet like me from your midst, from your brethren. Him you shall hear. (Deut 18: 15)

Whilst under the Roman Empire, this and many other texts prompted a great Jewish Messianic expectation in the first century. Sadly, many Jewish people did not realise that Jesus was not only their Messiah, but also the Saviour of the world, even the Gentiles.

Paul, at this point, took a most unusual step. His prime purpose was the concern he had for Agrippa, Festus and all his listeners. The defendant had resumed his role as a Gospel preacher. It is a quality rare, even amongst Christians, the priority of the salvation of others rather than his own freedom.

Festus by this time had had enough. He felt distinctly uncomfortable. He did not want his world-view to be ruffled, and then all he could say was that Paul's learning was driving Paul to madness. It seems that critics are full of excuses. At first, the comment made against the apostles was that they were unlearned men, and then the complaint was that Paul was too learned. Jesus was all too aware of the excuses of rejection:

We played the flute for you, And you did not dance; We mourned to you, And you did not lament. For John came neither eating nor drinking, and they say, 'He has a demon.' The Son of Man came eating and drinking, and they say, 'Look, a glutton and a winebibber, a friend of tax collectors and sinners!' But wisdom is justified by her children. (Mt 11:17-19)

Paul explained that he was thinking quite sanely, coherently and rationally. He then turned his attention to Agrippa, and made his appeal to him to change and become a Christian, on the grounds of the question, "Do you believe the prophets?"

The Greek at this point implies that Agrippa was almost persuaded, but most translators suggest that he was speaking sarcastically. The pride of worldly position and power was more precious to him than the kingdom of God, and identification with these despised Christians.

Centuries earlier, Moses had a similar choice, but he took the way of faith:

By faith Moses, when he became of age, refused to be called the son of Pharaoh's daughter, choosing rather to suffer affliction with the people of God than to enjoy the passing pleasures of sin, esteeming the reproach of Christ greater riches than the treasures in Egypt; for he looked to the reward. (Heb 11: 24-26)

Paul hoped that these officials would change and become believers like him, except for the chains that bound him. He also had thoughts for all his listeners, and maybe some of their hearts were touched. As the court dispersed, Agrippa's suggestion that Paul could have been released was somewhat hollow since he must have been aware of the threats made by Paul's accusers.

Before we leave this passage, it is doubtful that either Festus or Agrippa ever heard the gospel again. Festus's health soon broke and he died two years after, perhaps due to the strain of work. Agrippa, on the other hand, died many years later. It is important to respond to the gospel while there is an opportunity.

Acts 27:1-26

1 And when it was decided that we should sail to Italy, they delivered Paul and some other prisoners to one named Julius, a centurion of the Augustan Regiment. 2 So, entering a ship of Adramyttium, we put to sea, meaning to sail along the coasts of Asia. Aristarchus, a Macedonian of Thessalonica, was with us. 3 And the next day we landed at Sidon. And Julius treated Paul kindly and gave him liberty to go to his friends and receive care. 4 When we had put to sea from there, we sailed under the shelter of Cyprus, because the winds were contrary. 5 And when we had sailed over the sea which is off Cilicia and Pamphylia, we came to Myra, a city of Lycia. 6 There the centurion found an Alexandrian ship sailing to Italy, and he put us on board. 7 When we had sailed slowly many days, and arrived with difficulty off Cnidus, the wind not permitting us to proceed, we sailed under the shelter of Crete off Salmone. 8 Passing it with difficulty, we came to a place called Fair Havens, near the city of Lasea. 9 Now when much time had been spent, and sailing was now dangerous because the Fast was already over, Paul advised them, 10 saying, "Men, I perceive that this voyage will end with disaster and much loss, not only of the cargo and ship, but also our lives." 11 Nevertheless the centurion was more persuaded by the helmsman and the owner of the ship than by the things spoken by Paul. 12 And because the harbor was not suitable to winter in, the majority advised to set sail from there also, if by any means they could reach Phoenix, a harbor of Crete opening toward the southwest and northwest, and winter there. 13 When the south wind blew softly, supposing that they had obtained their desire, putting out to sea, they sailed close by Crete. 14 But not long after, a tempestuous head wind arose, called Euroclydon. 15 So when the ship was caught, and could not head into the wind, we let her drive. 16 And running under the shelter of an island called Clauda, we secured the skiff with difficulty. 17 When they had taken it on board, they used cables to undergird the ship; and fearing lest they should run aground on the Syrtis Sands, they struck sail and so were driven. 18 And because we were exceedingly tempest-tossed, the next day they lightened the ship. 19 On the third day we threw the ship's tackle overboard with our own hands. 20 Now when neither sun nor stars appeared for many days, and no small tempest beat on us, all hope that we would be saved was finally given up. 21 But after long abstinence from food, then Paul stood in the midst of them and said, "Men, you should have listened to me, and not have sailed from Crete and incurred this disaster and loss. 22 And now I

urge you to take heart, for there will be no loss of life among you, but only of the ship. 23 For there stood by me this night an angel of the God to whom I belong and whom I serve, 24 saying, 'Do not be afraid, Paul; you must be brought before Caesar; and indeed God has granted you all those who sail with you.' 25 Therefore take heart, men, for I believe God that it will be just as it was told me. 26 However, we must run aground on a certain island.

This chapter begins with three people who are to accompany Paul on a long sea voyage to Rome. The first is Luke, as indicated by the term 'we'. Luke had stayed in Caesarea, directing Paul's support. It is also possible that he took the opportunity to collect material for his Gospel, and subsequent "Acts". The other companion was Aristarchus who was nearly lynched in Ephesus. In a later epistle, he is referred to as, "my fellow prisoner". (Col 4:10) Not only were these men friends, but also it is clear from this narrative and elsewhere that they were loyal and tough and courageous. They knew hardship and did not shrink from it. The church is always in need of men like Luke and Aristarchus.

Julius, the centurion, is the last-named centurion in the Bible. The centurions described in the New Testament were all, no doubt, no-nonsense, sometimes ruthless men. Jesus was kind to soldiers and many of them responded to the gospel. Julius was a pagan and showed kindness to Paul, his most unusual prisoner.

Paul and the Christians of Sidon must have been delighted at the opportunity to share fellowship. For Paul, it was the first visit to a congregation for over two years. Thank God there is kindness in the world, even from the most unlikely sources. Julius gave to Paul and his companions a small measure of freedom. We are not told but it is possible that at some stage during the voyage Julius became a Christian. Intriguing as it is, the Bible does not tell us and we just do not know.

The slow progress of the ship along the Eastern and Northern Mediterranean coast late in the season indicated the possibility of looming disaster. Paul had undertaken many sea voyages, and no doubt, being the man he was, took a great interest in and learnt a lot about seamanship and navigation. Winter sailing was dangerous, as we know from today's loss of life amongst refugees who attempt the perilous journey from Africa to Europe.

In spite of Paul's warnings, the centurion listened to an inexperienced pilot and the ship owner, who wanted quick financial reward from the sale of his cargo. In addition, it was easier to secure the other prisoners on board ship rather than have the possibility of escape whilst on land. Clearly, it is good not to take unnecessary risks, even if it means delay.

The account of the storm at sea is one of the most vivid descriptions in the whole of ancient literature. The crew took various measures in order to prevent disaster. Good as they were, they were not of themselves sufficient.

From the next part of the story we notice some interesting details.

Firstly, as in other crises in Paul's life, he was aware of God's presence and advice. (v 23)

Secondly, we see Paul's natural gifts of leadership, combined with serene Christian faith. Although others were panicking and terrified, he trusted in the God who told him that they would all be saved. Paul asserted his authority by reminding them of his earlier warning not to sail. Instead of it being a chiding, "I told you so," it was there to reassure his hearers of his understanding of the situation.

Thirdly, Paul was more than willing to share the nature of his faith with others. Once again we hear the comforting words that echo through the Gospels and Acts, "Do not be afraid!"

Fourthly, we are reminded that our God is a gracious God who is with us whatever happens. Paul's advice to take courage was not an empty remark but based on the promises of God.

Fifthly, it is worth noting that, in effect, Paul was taking over command of the ship. When a captive in Philippi, he appeared to take control of the prison. When in the courtroom, he dominated the scene to the extent that Felix trembled. On the ship during the acute crisis of the storm, he appeared to take over. We may not have Paul's gifts, but we must not underestimate the moral authority of the gospel and the power of the indwelling Holy Spirit.

Acts 27:27-28:6

27 Now when the fourteenth night had come, as we were driven up and down in the Adriatic Sea, about midnight the sailors sensed that they were drawing near some land. **28** And they took soundings and found it to be twenty fathoms; and when they had gone a little farther, they took soundings again and found it to be fifteen fathoms. **29** Then, fearing lest we should run aground on the rocks, they dropped four anchors from the stern, and prayed for day to come. **30** And as the sailors were seeking to escape from the ship, when they had let down the skiff into the sea, under pretense of putting out anchors from the prow, **31** Paul said to the centurion and the soldiers, "Unless these men stay in the ship, you cannot be saved." **32** Then the soldiers cut away the ropes of the skiff and let it fall off. **33** And as day was about to dawn, Paul implored them all to take food, saying, "Today is the fourteenth day you have waited and continued without food, and eaten nothing. **34** Therefore I urge you to take nourishment, for this is for your survival, since not a hair will fall from the head of any of you." **35** And when he had said these things, he took bread and gave thanks to God in the presence of them all; and when he had broken it he began to eat. **36** Then they were all encouraged, and also took food themselves. **37** And in all we were two hundred and seventy-six persons on the ship. **38** So when they had eaten enough, they lightened the ship and threw out the wheat into the sea. **39** When it was day, they did not recognize the land; but they observed a bay with a beach, onto which they planned to run the ship if possible. **40** And they let go the anchors and left them in the sea, meanwhile loosing the rudder ropes; and they hoisted the mainsail to the wind and made for shore. **41** But striking a place where two seas met, they ran the ship aground; and the prow stuck fast and remained immovable, but the stern was being broken up by the violence of the waves. **42** And the soldiers' plan was to kill the prisoners, lest any of them should swim away and escape. **43** But the centurion, wanting to save Paul, kept them from their purpose, and commanded that those who could swim should jump overboard first and get to land, **44** and the rest, some on boards and some on parts of the ship. And so it was that they all escaped safely to land.

1 Now when they had escaped, they then found out that the island was called Malta. **2** And the natives showed us unusual kindness; for they kindled a fire and made us all welcome, because of the rain that was falling and because of the cold. 3 But when Paul had gathered a bundle of sticks and laid them on the fire, a viper came out because of the heat, and fastened on his hand. 4 So when the natives saw the creature hanging from his hand, they said to one another, "No doubt this man is a murderer, whom, though he has escaped the sea, yet justice does not allow to live." 5 But he shook off the creature into the fire and suffered no harm. 6 However, they were expecting that he would swell up or suddenly fall down dead. But after they had looked for a long time and saw no harm come to him, they changed their minds and said that he was a god.

The next part of the drama unfolds with an account of the desperation and selfish motivation of the sailors, and their attempt to escape in the lifeboat. The safety of the ship's occupants was no longer their priority. It was a case of, "me first", and, "every man for himself". Luke contrasted this with the attitude of Paul who wished for the safety of all on board.

After fourteen days of acute danger, constant suspense and lack of food, Paul invited everyone to eat. This showed his practical concern to prepare everyone for the final trial. Before he ate, he gave thanks to God, even in that desperate situation. Farmers may produce, retailers may distribute, cooks may prepare, and for that we should be grateful, but it is to God we must give thanks.

At last an island with a sandy beach was sighted. Then another crisis arose when the soldiers wanted to kill the prisoners, so that none should escape. Here Julius intervened. He wished to spare Paul's life and so ordered none to be harmed. Without doubt, it demonstrated his gratitude to Paul and his companions, but it also demonstrated God's sovereignty in the fulfilment of his promise that all 276 ship occupants would reach dry land. In spite of the break-up of the ship's stern when the ship was on the sand bank, all, including non-swimmers, were brought to safety.

The Maltese islanders were pagan and showed great kindness, which was notable in view of the large number of refugees. We should note that we all have things to learn from non-Christian friends and colleagues. Jesus was well aware of this. His take on this was surprising:

If you then, being evil, know how to give good gifts to your children, how much more will your heavenly Father give the Holy Spirit to those who ask Him! (Luke 11: 13)

It should be noted when ships have been wrecked on British coasts, the looters have taken what they could. In this instance, however, there was no loot to take, except the meagre belongings of a few individuals. The ship owner thought that great wealth would arise out of this journey. In fact, he lost everything. Again Jesus commented on such a situation:

Do not lay up for yourselves treasures on earth, where moth and rust destroy and where thieves break in and steal; but lay up for yourselves treasures in heaven, where neither moth nor rust destroys and where thieves do not break in and steal. For where your treasure is, there your heart will be also. (Mt 6: 19-21)

Millions use their worldly possessions and their status in order to push God out of their lives. This shipwreck demonstrates vividly that one day all will be gone.

Before leaving the account of the storm and shipwreck, some commentators have wondered why Luke should have devoted such a large section of Acts to this episode. There must be, they suggest, a theological reason or allegory behind it. A better explanation is that Luke was an eyewitness and wrote the details to demonstrate God's over-riding sovereignty and the fact that it really did happen. Wind, storms and towering waves are powerful forces, but God is still in control. He also knew that people in general love to read about real-life drama.

Although tired and hungry from the disaster, Paul, as ever practical, began to help make the fire. A snake attached itself to Paul's hand, which he quickly shook off. The locals first thought that as a prisoner, he must be a murderer and would not escape justice, then thought he must be a god because he showed no ill effects. As with many in the ancient world, and today, they had no idea of a transcendent creator God. Their gods were real and imagined created beings or images, which were changeable, capricious, and flawed. So too are the heroes of our modern cult of celebrity.

Acts 28:7-16

7 In that region there was an estate of the leading citizen of the island, whose name was Publius, who received us and entertained us courteously for three days. **8** And it happened that the father of Publius lay sick of a fever and dysentery. Paul went in to him and prayed, and he laid his hands on him and healed him. **9** So when this was done, the rest of those on the island who had diseases also came and were healed. **10** They also honored us in many ways; and when we departed, they provided such things as were necessary. **11** After three months we sailed in an Alexandrian ship whose figurehead was the Twin Brothers, which had wintered at the island. **12** And landing at Syracuse, we stayed three days. **13** From there we circled round and reached Rhegium. And after one day the south wind blew; and the next day we came to Puteoli, **14** where we found brethren, and were invited to stay with them seven days. And so we went toward Rome. **15** And from there, when the brethren heard about us, they came to meet us as far as Appii Forum and Three Inns. When Paul saw them, he thanked God and took courage. **16** Now when we came to Rome, the centurion delivered the prisoners to the captain of the guard; but Paul was permitted to dwell by himself with the soldier who guarded him.

The notable hospitality of Publius, the chief official, must have been welcome to Paul and his friends. After years of captivity, at last the bed was comfortable and the food, very agreeable. Paul had learnt so much about God's provision over the years:

I know how to be abased, and I know how to abound. Everywhere and in all things I have learned both to be full and to be hungry, both to abound and to suffer need. I can do all things through Christ who strengthens me. (Phil 4: 12 -13)

Paul's ministry on the island was a healing ministry, a ministry which arose at various times in his life. Publius must have been so grateful when his father was healed. We must be ready to visit our sick friends and pray with them. Although people may or may not be healed in a way we might wish, the Bible states that the prayer of a righteous man "avails much". (James 5: 16)

There appears to be no record of a teaching ministry on Malta, and this may have been because of the language difficulty. However, it is worth noting that Malta has maintained a Christian presence to this day, in spite of sieges and attempted invasions. Before leaving Malta, it must have been clear to all including the soldiers that Paul was not guilty of any crime, and like Jesus his master, he went around doing good.

After three months, sailing was possible, and the journey continued to Sicily, and then on to Italy. The figurehead at the front of the ship was more than mere decoration; it demonstrated the superstitious nature of seafarers.

It must have been marvellous for the three companions to find some Christians at Puteoli, where they spent a week. Paul often spent time alone, but he loved companionship. He loved to talk about the gospel and all the future projects for Christ that they would do together.

Soon after his arrival at Puteoli, some young lad was no doubt sent on ahead to tell the other believers of the apostle's pending arrival. Again, Paul was encouraged by the welcome he received at Appius and the Three Taverns. The people, to whom he had sent his great treatise on the faith, the Epistle to the Romans, nearly three years earlier, were there to welcome the travellers with warm greetings and fellowship. The way we greet people speaks volumes about our inner spiritual health. Paul would have also been encouraged by the way in which ordinary believers had spread the gospel. These people were like the men from Cyprus and Cyrene who spread the gospel in Syrian Antioch all those years earlier. (Acts 11: 20)

The arrival in Rome was not in the manner Paul had expected. His freedom was very limited, and he was in light chains, but he did have a house to live in and he could receive guests and talk to anyone and everyone. The gospel even moved into the elite of Rome's military machine. In spite of his confinement, Paul was happy and the gospel spread:

But I want you to know, brethren, that the things which happened to me have actually turned out for the furtherance of the gospel, so that it has become evident to the whole palace guard, and to all the rest, that my chains are in Christ; and most of the brethren in the Lord, having become confident by my chains, are much more bold to speak the word without fear. (Phil 1: 12 -14)

Such is the paradox of the power of the gospel. In his last letter to Timothy, Paul asserted again that the word of God is not chained. (2 Tim 2: 9)

Acts 28:17-31

17 And it came to pass after three days that Paul called the leaders of the Jews together. So when they had come together, he said to them: "Men and brethren, though I have done nothing against our people or the customs of our fathers, yet I was delivered as a prisoner from Jerusalem into the hands of the Romans, **18** who, when they had examined me, wanted to let me go, because there was no cause for putting me to death. **19** But when the Jews spoke against it, I was compelled to appeal to Caesar, not that I had anything of which to accuse my nation. **20** For this reason therefore I have called for you, to see you and speak with you, because for the hope of Israel I am bound with this chain." **21** Then they said to him, "We neither received letters from Judea concerning you, nor have any of the brethren who came reported or spoken any evil of you. **22** But we desire to hear from you what you think; for concerning this sect, we know that it is spoken against everywhere." **23** So when they had appointed him a day, many came to him at his lodging, to whom he explained and solemnly testified of the kingdom of God, persuading them concerning Jesus from both the Law of Moses and the Prophets, from morning till evening. **24** And some were persuaded by the things which were spoken, and some disbelieved. **25** So when they did not agree among themselves, they departed after Paul had said one word: "The Holy Spirit spoke rightly through Isaiah the prophet to our fathers, **26** saying, 'Go to this people and say: "Hearing you will hear, and shall not understand; And seeing you will see, and not perceive; **27** For the hearts of this people have grown dull. Their ears are hard of hearing, And their eyes they have closed, Lest they should see with their eyes and hear with their ears, Lest they should understand with their hearts and turn, So that I should heal them." **28** "Therefore let it be known to you that the salvation of God has been sent to the Gentiles, and they will hear it!" **29** And when he had said these words, the Jews departed and had a great dispute among themselves. **30** Then Paul dwelt two whole years in his own rented house, and received all who came to him, **31** preaching the kingdom of God and teaching the things which concern the Lord Jesus Christ with all confidence, no one forbidding him.

Three days after his arrival, Paul moved into action again. The apostle called the Jewish leaders together for a conference. There are some items from this meeting that are worth noting.

Firstly, we see the straightforward honesty and transparency of Paul in his reasons for his arrival in Rome as a prisoner. Everything he said about the court process and that he was not considered guilty of any crime was completely true. He then moved to his real motivation, "the hope of Israel". (v 20)

Secondly, we notice the response of the Jewish leaders who claimed not to have heard bad reports about Paul, but here comes the sting. "People everywhere are talking against this sect." (v 21) Christians are frequently criticised as "the God squad", or "God botherers", and the real insult is that you hold a certain view on an issue because of your religion. The jibe about the latter is that to hold a Christian perspective is against reason and is an out-of-date way of thinking. They ignore the fact that Christians seek to do things out of compassion, and are the most likely to give to charities. Jesus received unjust criticism, and warned that the same thing would happen to Christians.

The third thing we notice is that Paul and the leaders were prepared to spend a whole day in discussion. Few of us would be prepared or able to carry on for such a length of time. Nevertheless, the church needs to cultivate men and women who can do just that. Reasoning for the faith is not the most fruitful source of converts, but it is a source, and gives reassurance to believers who find themselves in the company of intellectual critics.

Fourthly, not for the first time, Paul made his way through the Hebrew Scriptures, in order to demonstrate that Jesus of Nazareth was truly the Messiah, sent from God, to His people. Once again, there was disagreement amongst the assembly. Some believed and some did not. Some accepted and some did not. Such was and is the effect of gospel preaching.

The quote from Isaiah is a sad reflection on those who repeatedly hear the gospel and yet remain unmoved. Jesus quoted the same passage when he explained the Parable of the Sower. (Mt 13:14-15)

Preachers are aware of the phenomenon of those who hear the gospel year after year and seem to become increasingly hardened. Although this is true in the main, there are the exceptions of those who convert in later life and who then wonder why ever they had not responded earlier.

Finally, Acts begins with a reference to the risen Christ teaching His disciples about the kingdom of God. The final verse speaks about Paul preaching boldly about the kingdom of God and Jesus Christ. Jesus insisted that His kingdom was not of this world, in the sense of political authority. However, it would not be too long before there was a clash with the cult practices associated with emperor worship. Christians, who refused to take part in these practices, were to be the recipients of severe persecution at the hands of a brutal Roman Empire.

The kingdom is about the past, present and future. However, the contents of Acts reveal much about the kingdom as lived out here in this world. It is a kingdom where Christ reigns in the hearts of His believers. The leaders are respected but believers are prepared to deny themselves and suffer for the sake of that kingdom. It is a kingdom, which may mean martyrdom, as happened to some early Christians, including Stephen and James. It is a kingdom, which acknowledges the death and resurrection of Jesus. It is a kingdom of new beginnings and transformation, as in the case of Paul and so many others. It is a kingdom of fellowship and care for others, which warmed the hearts of multitudes.

I like a saying of William Tyndale, the early Bible translator:

Euangelio (that we call gospel) is a Greek word and signifieth good, merry, glad and joyful tidings, that maketh man's heart glad, and maketh him sing, dance and leap for joy.

Acts ends abruptly, and leaves us wanting more, but it is all we need to take heart in our day-to-day Christian experience.